INDIA'S FREEDOM STORY

First published in India in 2021 by HarperCollins Children's Books

An imprint of HarperCollins *Publishers*

A-75, Sector 57, Noida, Uttar Pradesh 201301, India

www.harpercollins.co.in

2 4 6 8 10 9 7 5 3 1

P-ISBN 978-93-5489-256-1
E-ISBN 978-93-5489-263-9

Layout and design in Alegreya 10pt/15 by Sukriti Sobti

Printed and bound at Replika Press Pvt. Ltd.

FSC
www.fsc.org
MIX
Paper from
responsible sources
FSC® C016779

INDIA'S FREEDOM STORY

IRA SAXENA & NILIMA SINHA

ILLUSTRATED BY ARUN POTTIRAYIL
DESIGNED BY SUKRITI SOBTI

HarperCollins*Children's Books*

To Bapu,
the eternal spirit of nonviolence

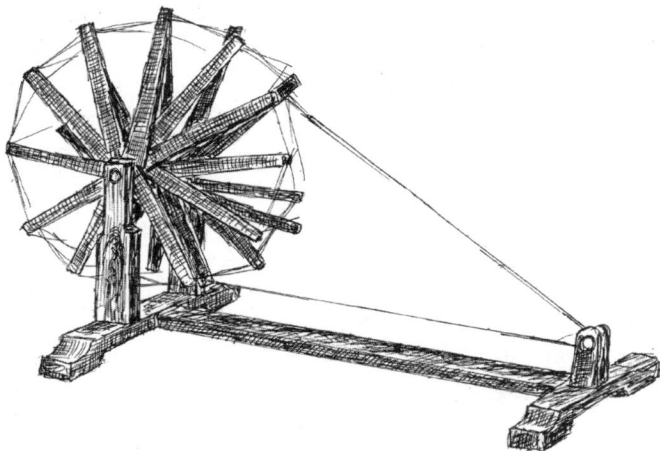

PRAISE FOR THE BOOK

"This book relays around three words – freedom, victory and nonviolence. Freedom is an inviolable right. The book critically examines basic rights such as liberty, justice and equality. I wish to congratulate the authors for having penned down their thoughts based on actual happenings during India's freedom struggle."

Anil Shastri, politician, Congress leader,
son of former Prime Minister Lal Bahadur Shastri

"The book is a candid recreation of long-colonised Indians' gradual awakening to the idea of freedom as their birthright and the long freedom movement that followed. The struggle led by Gandhi swung between glory and tragedy but remained remarkably nonviolent on the Indian side. The young adults whom this book addresses have not witnessed the struggle but will find that it also addresses today's issues. After the destruction and violence witnessed across the world, including our own country, it is refreshing to recall Gandhi's contribution to our freedom struggle that was driven by a compelling passion for reconciliation and peaceful resolution of old conflicts between communities."

Mrinal Pande, author and journalist

AUTHOR'S NOTE

The saga of India's struggle for freedom stands out in the annals of world history like an anthem echoing the message of nonviolence, peace and democratic co-existence.

The pages of this book unfold the unique struggle for India's freedom in a chronological sequence, as we recount the thrilling drama of the triumph of nonviolence in attaining this freedom. Under the dynamic leadership of Mahatma Gandhi, our freedom fighters demonstrated the inner strength of a moral force, courage and spirit of self-sacrifice.

We hope this book will present an inspiring picture for our young readers of the heroism and sacrifices made by Indians in attaining freedom from the British. The book will also highlight changemakers and contemporary struggles from the rest of the world.

We hope this book will show readers that the weapon of nonviolence is not for the weak. Our hope is that the sacrifices of our freedom heroes will help the young in fighting for their own freedoms in a world mired in conflict and chaos.

The book will also touch upon other contemporary movements from around the world that follow Gandhi's message of nonviolence.

As India completes 75 years of Independence, it is a good time to look back and celebrate the extraordinary stories that brought us this freedom.

Personal tributes from the authors:

"*My heart swells with pride as I remember my mother, Kamala Chaudhri, a freedom fighter, poet and writer who was elected to the Constituent Assembly and later joined the Lok Sabha. Her beliefs transformed my father, Dr. J.M.Chaudhri, who became her resolute supporter, in the true spirit of swadeshi. She followed the dictates of Gandhi, practicing Satyagraha devotedly and restoring peace before Partition. Through the stories shared by her about the freedom movement, I developed a keen insight into the tumultuous period enabling me to feel the determination of people to endure and suffer for the sake of freedom. Her words have been the true source of inspiration in writing this book to fulfil my mother's desire to narrate the story of our freedom struggle for the youth of our nation.*"

Ira Saxena

"*I am grateful to my father, NC Shrivastava (ICS), who, during his posting in Shimla, took me to a meeting where I was thrilled to see Gandhiji in person. Later my father was posted to Delhi with the specific responsibility of resettling refugees after the Partition. As a child residing in Delhi, I was able to witness the arrival of Freedom, and also experienced the turmoil that accompanied it. As a child, I remember the great shock we felt at the sudden death of Gandhiji, adored leader of the nation. I hope this book makes a fascinating read for today's children, who may be unaware of the emotional ups and downs of those days.*"

Nilima Sinha

CONTENTS

The then Prime Minister Jawaharlal Nehru signing the Constitution of India in New Delhi, on 24th January 1950.

INTRODUCTION

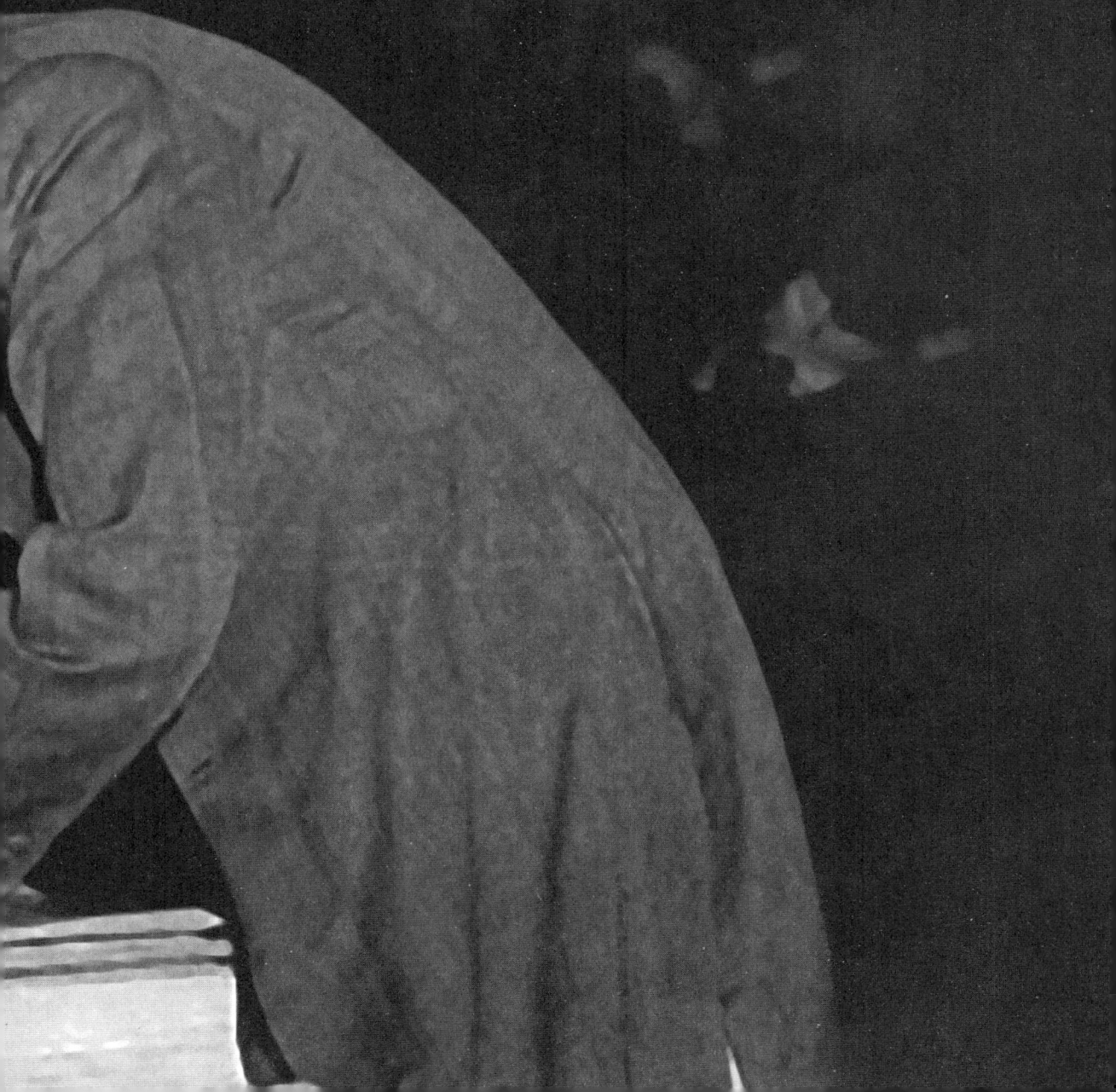

THE IDEA OF FREEDOM

Freedom may have many meanings, depending on an individual and his or her desires. No one can be happy in bondage. All of us need the freedom to be ourselves, to live life as we like, in a way that satisfies and makes us happy.

According to some scriptures, the aim of a human being is to find happiness through the search for truth, by realizing one's full potential. Freedom to develop, to progress and to find happiness is therefore essential to all human beings.

Through the ages, many rulers have tried to curb the free spirit of their subjects. Wars have been fought and nations destroyed to subjugate the free spirit of others. However, long ago, Indian thinkers had discovered that this spirit was universal, all pervading and, most importantly, indestructible. People rose time and again, to fight for their right to freedom. For no human can ever be happy in enslavement.

Thinkers, philosophers and leaders were the first to recognise the importance of freedom and have struggled to attain it for their people. They fought wars and led revolutions. History bears witness to the fact that whenever an existing system becomes unbearable to the vast majority of people, it is overthrown by those suffering the oppression. Change has been brought about by force or peaceful means, depending on the character and maturity of the people.

Politically speaking, for a nation and its citizens, the rules formed to govern a free country include well-defined promises which guarantee that each citizen is free to lead the life that she or he wants.

However, freedom does not give the right to go against accepted social norms of the time or to commit crimes against others. Freedom also entails responsibility.

RIGHT TO FREEDOM

Today, as a free nation, we have the rights to Liberty, Justice and Equality. All of us as citizens of a free nation have several other rights that are enshrined in the Constitution, drafted by our leaders. The Constitution lays down the laws of the country and each of us, including the government, is duty bound to uphold these rules, which ensure the welfare of all citizens. Our Constitution protects these rights to make sure that each person has the freedom to live without fear.

For a country like India, with its diverse population from various religions and castes, several aspects needed to be considered before rules could be framed to benefit each of its citizens. One can only imagine how difficult it would have been to reach the right conclusions and draft rules for a country as massive and diverse as India. It is no wonder that it took so long (three years) to draft the Constitution. Changes to this document continue to be made to this day.

These words, written in the Preamble to our Constitution, were included to make sure that each citizen of this nation is free to progress and develop as she or he desires, and the spirit of the individual remains free.

Some of the promises made to the nation include Right to Equality before the Law, Right to Freedom of Speech, Right Against Exploitation, Right to Freedom of Religion, Culture and Education, Right to Property and Right to Justice.

As citizens of India, we are all equal before the law. Men or women, rich or poor, irrespective of class, caste, religion or region; we are all equal and have the same rights. No individual can be sentenced without a proper trial in a court. We have the right to own property and possessions that cannot be taken away from us. We are free to express ourselves through personal speech or the press. Nobody has the right to exploit us. We can practice our religion and develop our culture the way we like. Each of us has the right to education, right to jobs, right to travel and right to live where we prefer. If these rights, promised by our Constitution, are denied to us, we can appeal to the courts.

As a democratic nation, each adult citizen– again irrespective of sex, class, caste, religion or region– has the right to cast his or her vote during elections, to elect members that represent him in the panchayat, municipality,

THE CONSTITUTION OF INDIA

Preamble.

WE, THE PEOPLE OF INDIA, having solemnly resolved to constitute India into a **SOVEREIGN DEMOCRATIC REPUBLIC** and to secure to all its citizens:

JUSTICE, social, economic and political;

LIBERTY of thought, expression, belief, faith and worship;

EQUALITY of status and of opportunity;

and to promote among them all

FRATERNITY assuring the dignity of the individual and the unity of the Nation;

IN OUR CONSTITUENT ASSEMBLY this twenty-sixth day of November, 1949, do **HEREBY ADOPT, ENACT AND GIVE TO OURSELVES THIS CONSTITUTION.**

state assembly, or in Parliament. If these representatives do nothing for a citizen's welfare, he or she is free not to vote for him or her in the next election.

The elected representatives at the Parliamentary level run the government through the executive. They discuss and enact laws in the legislatures. Some of them form the government and control the administration. If these members fail to protect the rights or do not run the administration according to the wishes of the citizens, the latter have the freedom to change the government by not voting for them again. Thus, we are free to elect or remove a government if it does not work for our welfare.

However, these rights cannot be taken for granted. There was a time when we did not have many of these rights. We could not change the government even when it did not protect our rights. We were forced to bear the yoke of our rulers when India was under the rule of the British Crown. We were a subject nation whose people were treated as second-class citizens in their own country. Humiliations and degradations such as not being eligible to serve in the highest ranks or being kept away from first-class coaches in the railways were thrust upon Indians.

But today, as free citizens of an independent nation, we can hold our heads high in front of other nations, and live with dignity as people who are in no way inferior to others.

For this, we must thank the generation which fought to win this precious freedom.

Thousands of courageous men and women struggled and died for this cause. The struggle went on for almost a century and was won at the end, not through war and bloodshed, but by using the unique weapon of ahimsa or nonviolence. Nonviolence is not the weapon of the weak. Only the most courageous can practice this for it requires a strong and fearless spirit to face force with love and tolerance.

This is why we admire our freedom heroes and their story, which is more fascinating than any modern-day thriller. Let us begin by turning the pages of history to catch a glimpse of British-ruled India.

The British East India Company landed on the Indian Subcontinent at the port of Surat on 24th August 1608 for the purpose of trade. The Company was formed in 1599.

ARRIVAL OF THE BRITISH

1707 Death of Aurangzeb • **1757** Battle of Plassey • **1784** East India Company Act • **1849** Naga Revolt

India was once known for its riches and great wealth. Tales of the wonderful treasures to be found here spread all over the world. Travellers and adventurers set out to discover this "land of gold". Lured by accounts of the riches found in this glorious land, several travellers from Europe had arrived on the Indian shores in the 17th century. French, Portuguese and British traders belonging to the East India Company began to trade with India. When Aurangzeb, the last of the great Mughal rulers, died in 1707, there was chaos and confusion in the country. The successive Mughal emperors were too weak to keep their control over a country as vast as India. In such conditions whoever was most powerful managed to rule.

The Marathas dominated in the West. In the South, Hyder Ali, followed by Tipu Sultan, were supreme, as were the Sikhs under Ranjit Singh in Punjab. The eastern region saw the emergence of the nawabs in Bengal and Bihar.

BATTLE OF PLASSEY

Foreign trading companies such as the East India Company also joined in this struggle to seize power. In those days anybody could enlist men to fight for money as there was no national army in India. In order to protect its settlements, the East India Company employed and maintained a well-trained and disciplined army. At first, the British used it to put down rival traders like the French and the Portuguese. Later, they began to lend this army to the various rulers engaged in waging wars against each other. Lord Robert Clive, who later went on to become the first Governor-General of the Bengal Presidency, led the army and conquered several states.

In 1757, the Battle of Plassey brought the eastern parts of India under foreign rule through a major victory against the nawabs of Bengal and Bihar. The wealth gained proved an incentive to control more territory.

Lord Richard Wellesley, who was appointed

the Governor-General to look after Indian affairs by the East India Company, continued the onward march of British rule and succeeded in winning over the rulers of several other princely states in the rest of the country. For this, he formulated the policy of "subsidiary alliances". He made them the allies of the British and gave them the protection of the Company, in return for large sums of money.

James Andrew Broun-Ramsay, better known as Lord Dalhousie, went several steps further in his quest for more territory. He annexed the kingdoms of Satara, Nagpur, Punjab, Jhansi, Awadh and others under his policy of "Doctrine of Lapse". It was a clever ploy to snatch property from the rulers. Using this unfair policy, Lord Dalhousie seized the lands of Indian rulers whenever they died without leaving sons as heirs. Despite the then prevailing custom of adopting sons, the English refused to recognize adopted children as heirs.

Battle of Plassey, 1757

EAST INDIA COMPANY

By the mid-19th century, the British, by using a combination of force and sly tactics, had established themselves as a major power in India. The East India Company was a purely commercial enterprise whose work was to trade with the East. Its officers, who came to be known as "nabobs", acquired vast fortunes through unfair trade practices and forcible collection of bribes and gifts from Indian chiefs and rulers. They exploited and oppressed the people.

In 1784, under the Pitt's India Act (also known as the East India Company Act), control over the Company and its affairs in India was taken over by the British government. Through various other acts, the British government took over full control of the East India Company. The Governor-General became the supreme authority and the real effective ruler of India. No Indians were allowed to participate in the administration of their own country.

East India Company Coat of Arms

The British government introduced their own systems and completely overhauled the administration of areas under their rule. The army, the police and the civil services maintained law and order to keep peace in the country, for without peace they could not sell or buy to make profit. The British made full use of their superior force in controlling the Indians. To get rid of bribery and corruption, the officers were given much higher salaries, making the civil servicemen the most privileged lot at that time. The government did not trust Indians to look after the interests of the Englishmen and kept them out. The army protected the British Empire not only from foreign rivals but also against chiefs and rulers within the country. Laws and courts were established, but justice was too costly and complicated to be of use to the poor.

PLUNDER AND PROFIT

The aim of the British rule was to make as much profit as possible from India, without thinking of the effect of its policies on the Indian people. The economic policies of the British government soon reduced the country to poverty and despair. The rich and vast resources of the country were exploited by merchants and traders to gain wealth for themselves and for Britain. Raw materials like cotton, silk, indigo, food grains, iron and tea were shipped to Britain. Once manufactured into finished products in English factories, they were re-sold in India. No import duties were levied on these mill-made goods in India. Indian handmade goods, on the other hand, were taxed when traders tried to sell them outside India. Indian handicrafts and handmade goods could not compete with the cheaper mill-made imported products, leading to a sharp decline in their sales. Forced to give up work, Indian artisans and craftspersons were pushed into poverty.

Wealth was also drained due to the high salaries paid to British officers, who carried back home huge amounts of money. A substantial amount was also spent on maintaining the army.

Nearly six million pounds were transferred from India to England between 1758 and 1776 A.D.

The agrarian policies of the government added to the drain and increased the misery of the people. Besides making huge profits through trade, money was collected in the form of land revenues from areas under the British. This made the British greedy for more territory. The government then started to extort maximum land revenue from the peasants, either directly or through zamindars, by imposing very high rates. Both the zamindars and the peasants suffered at the hands of the British. Many zamindars could not afford to pay high rent due to droughts or famines. The failure to pay resulted in the seizure of their lands by the British. Peasants were left at the mercy of the zamindars who treated them most unjustly.

In addition to all their economic troubles, the loss of prestige and dignity added to the people's fury. Feudal lords, till recently the masters of their land, were reduced to underlings and subjected to insults and humiliation. Nobles, nawabs and princes could no longer maintain their lavish lifestyles. Artists and performers also lost the patronage and shelter of the royal courts. Their suffering led to discontentment with the British rule.

To add to all this, missionaries tried to impose their own religion on the people. The scorn and contempt shown by them towards Indian religions and customs only added insult to injury. Both Hindus and Muslims were perturbed by the threat to their religions and traditions.

The soldiers employed by the British army were treated most shabbily, despite the fact that these Indian sepoys had fought loyally and helped the British conquer India. Compared to the English, the salaries of Indian sepoys were very low. Not only this, their status and living conditions were inferior to British sepoys of the same level. Indians had become servants of the British masters in their own home.

Helpless in the face of British power and force, Indians were robbed of their power and prestige. Their old, traditional way of life had been destroyed, reducing them to faceless serfs with the sole purpose of serving their foreign ruler.

It was then a matter of time when the oppressed would rise to break these chains, leading to a series of outbreaks in various parts of the country.

Cargo ships carrying goods

EARLY VOICES OF DISSENT

In the South, the Rajas of Malabar openly defied the British. Kerala Varma, Raja of Kottayam dynasty, defeated the British thrice. In Assam, the British were attacked by a chief in 1830. The Nagas revolted in 1849. There were similar revolts by the chiefs of various princely states in Bundelkhand. Small revolts continued to erupt every now and then in the country.

The most remarkable of these early rebellions was the Sanyasi Revolt. The "Sanyasis", an organization of Hindu and Muslim fakirs, fought several times against British forces and were not easy to subdue. Operating in Bengal and Bihar, the sanyasis raided English factories and government treasuries. The uprising went on for about 50 years and was completely suppressed by the 1820s.

In Punjab, Sayed Ahmed of Rae Bareli organized a great revolt against the foreign rulers. His followers, known as the Wahabis, had their headquarters in Patna, from where they continued to fight for many years. People from various tribes also fought to protect their own way of life. The Khasis of Assam, Khonds of Orissa, Bhils of Khandesh and several other tribes refused to be subdued. In Chhota Nagpur, Santals, led by two brothers Sidhu and Kanu, declared war against the British in 1855. Birsa Munda was another freedom fighter from the Adivasi community who rose against the British. The adivasis had to surrender after fierce fighting, in which a number of Britishers were killed. Ruthless and cruel treatment was meted out to these tribals as punishment.

The British succeeded in subduing all these attempts through their superior strength and power. However, they were not the first outsiders to establish their rule over India. Invaders and conquerors had come before, some to loot and plunder, and others to rule. But previous rulers like the Lodhis, the Khiljis and the Mughals had stayed here and become part of the vast and variegated life of the nation. However, the Britishers, who came as traders but stayed on to rule, never tried to become one with the people. They remained aloof. Their only aim was to derive maximum profit from this country. No efforts were made to improve the condition of the people. Britain flourished, while India, drained of all resources, sank into a quagmire of suffering, misery, ignorance and poverty.

After the victory at the Battle of Koonch, Sir Hugh Rose advanced towards Kalpi, where Tantia Tonpe gave him a tough fight.

THE GREAT INDIAN
UPRISING

1764 British Win Battle of Buxar
• **1857** First War of Independence • **1857** Execution of
Mangal Pandey • **1857** British Seize Red Fort

The discontent and anger felt everywhere made the whole country simmer with hatred against the new rulers. According to some historians, disinherited nawabs and princes like Nana Sahib of Bithur, the rulers of Awadh, Jhansi and Jagdishpur, and even the old king Bahadur Shah Zafar of Delhi plotted a war against the foreign rule. They laid out careful and well-organized plans for a great uprising across the country. The date set for the big revolt was 31st May 1857.

Secret, coded messages were sent to every corner of the country, asking as many people as possible to join in the war. Encrypted notes were exchanged among the sepoys employed by the British through chapatis (Indian flatbread), which appeared "mysteriously" in various towns and villages. The message was clear: Prepare for a massive battle to drive away the British.

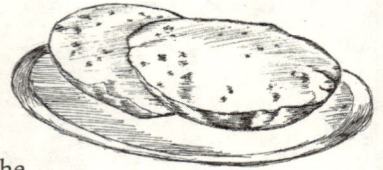

INDIA'S FIRST WAR OF INDEPENDENCE

While some historians believe that all these acts of rebellion did take place, a few others remain doubtful.

Before this plan could be carried out, something else happened to fan the simmering discontent into a blazing fire of open revolt. The flames of this fire were to spread through the length and breadth of the country and thousands were to perish

The Enfield rifle and greased cartridges

in what came to be known as India's First War of Independence.

Around this time, the British introduced a new weapon, called the Enfield rifle, which was to be used by the sepoys. The cartridges of this rifle were greased with fat from animals such as cow and pig. The ends of these cartridges had to be bitten off before firing the rifles. The Muslim and Hindu sepoys in the British Army refused to use the new weapon as it hurt their religious sensibilities. Instead of respecting their religious beliefs, the British officers tried to force them to carry out the orders. The lack of consideration angered the soldiers and their fury soon led to a revolt after months of protests by the Bengal Army since early 1857.

Company, stationed at Barrackpore near Calcutta. At first, he tried to persuade his comrades to join him in the protest. When they remained undecided, he firmly held his gun and jumped boldly on to the parade ground, shouting out to the others to join him. As soon as the British officer, Lieutenant Baugh, ran out to see what was happening, Pandey fired at him. Lt. Baugh shot back but missed. Pandey ran towards the enemy, with the weapon in his hand. Realizing that he would soon be overpowered and captured by the British, Pandey shot himself. He was caught in a wounded state and sentenced to death. Pandey became an Indian martyr on 8th April 1857.

On 29th March 1857, a young soldier called Mangal Pandey finally lost his patience. He belonged to the 34th Bengal Native Infantry regiment of the East India

News of this bold and courageous act spread to distant barracks and inspired others to raise similar banners of revolt.

A fortnight after Pandey's death, on 24th April 1857, eighty-five men of the 3rd Bengal Light Cavalry Regiment posted in Meerut refused to touch the cartridges and were arrested. As a warning to others, the British officers decided to make a public show of the punishment. These men, otherwise a loyal and brave group, were stripped in front of a large crowd. The rebels were led to jail like serious offenders, with their hands and feet chained. Other sepoys, who were witnessing the grave injustice being done to their colleagues, felt their blood boil in helpless anger and resolved to avenge this insult.

On what seemed to be a regular Sunday in Meerut, with British officers out at church, the horsemen of the 3rd Bengal Light Cavalry sneaked into a prison and silently freed their fellow soldiers who had been arrested for defying the British. Soon after, the Indian horsemen rode back to kill the British officers who had humiliated their fellow sepoys. The soldiers went on a rampage and set the house of their British superiors on fire, and galloped out of Meerut.

Riding through the night, the fleeing horsemen reached the outskirts of Delhi by dawn. Taken by surprise, the British displayed no resistance and fled the city. Meanwhile, the Indian troops posted in Delhi joined their Meerut comrades. In triumph, they marched through the gates of the Red Fort and demanded to see the last Mughal King Bahadur Shah Zafar, who like many other rulers, had become a puppet in the hands of the British. The soldiers declared Bahadur Shah the Emperor of Hindustan and requested him to become their leader.

The whole incident acted as a spark that lighted a fire to inspire future rebellions. It acted as a signal for the countrymen to rise against the British. A series of revolts followed and spread to the rest of India. Inspired by the call for action, men in barracks killed their British officers and rode off to join the battle. Peasants and civilians too joined in the struggle wholeheartedly.

LORD CANNING

When Lord Canning, the British Governor-General in Calcutta, heard that Delhi had been captured, he immediately ordered troops to march towards the city. Canning regarded the capture of Delhi to be of great importance. Brigadier Archdale Wilson of Bengal Artillery in Meerut was the first one to arrive at Delhi in response to Canning's order. Wilson encountered the Indian soldiers on the banks of the River Hindon, near Delhi. Defeated by the British, the Indian soldiers retreated to Delhi. Wilson, joined by another officer called Barnard, fought them again in Badli-ki-Serai, five miles away from Delhi. After a fierce defence, the Indians took their position on the Ridge, from where they could get a good view of the whole city. From here, they kept up a fierce attack, making the British suffer heavy casualties. Inspite of their brave stand, the soldiers soon lost the Ridge to their enemy.

Driven into the city, the Indians made several attacks on their British foes. They had little funds, no food and insufficient ammunition, yet they stood their ground in Delhi for six long months. The fighting went on for long, with as many as twenty battles taking place in a month. The British Army was reinforced with fresh arrival of men, supplies and ammunition from Punjab. After fierce and heavy fighting, in which an important officer called Nicholson was killed, the British troops were able to enter Delhi. On 20th September 1857, Indian rebels took over the Lahori Gate, blew open the gates of the Red Fort and marched back into the city. Emperor Bahadur Shah, along with his wife Zeenat Mahal, who had actively helped the Indian soldiers in this cause, decided to flee to Humayun's Tomb. However, their guards were killed by the British and the royal fugitives were captured.

The two sons of Emperor Bahadur Shah were killed in the most cruel manner in front of their father. However, the British spared the king and the queen, who were deported from India to Burma.

BEGUM HAZRAT MAHAL OF AWADH

News of the uprising in Meerut and the first defeat of the British in Delhi reached Awadh, then a state in the United Provinces. It had been annexed only the previous year by Lord Dalhousie. The Nawab of Awadh, Wajid Ali Shah, had been exiled to Calcutta on the excuse that he was a bad ruler. His begum Hazrat Mahal and her eleven-year-old son Birjis Qadr were forced to live in Lucknow under impoverished conditions. This gave the people of Awadh another cause for anger against the British.

Sir Henry Lawrence, the officer-in-charge at Lucknow, realized that the soldiers posted in the city would soon respond to the call to fight. He chose a building on the banks of River Gomti, called the Residency, and moved the British ladies to safety behind its walls.

As expected, soldiers of Awadh rose to fight, and succeeded in establishing their control over the area. Begum Hazrat Mahal took over command on behalf of her son. Maulvi Ahmadulla, who advised her on military matters, helped her in this fight. When the Indian soldiers advanced to attack Lucknow, Sir Havelock marched forward to take on the rebels at a town called Chinhat. The fierce onslaught by the Indians forced the British to flee and take shelter in the Residency. However, the Indian sepoys soon laid siege. Located on an elevation, the Residency was guarded by soldiers who managed to fend off attacks by the British. This went on for nine long months. A continuous onslaught of gunshots and cannon attacks made things difficult for the Britishers caught inside. Several English officers, including Sir Henry, were killed. When the Indian soldiers ran short of ammunition, they resorted to firing bullets made of wood, pieces of iron and even bullock horns. The British responded with great force, dying in thousands while trying to defend the Residency.

The Residency at Lucknow was set up after the British won the Battle of Buxar in 1764 CE. In the battle, the third Nawab of Awadh Shuja-ud-Daula had formed an alliance with the then Nawab of Bengal Mir Qasim and Mughal emperor Shah Alam against the East India Company and lost badly. Following this, the Residency was handed over to the British. They appointed a Resident General who made the 33-acre plot in Lucknow his residence and office complex, and it came to be known as the "Residency".

Soon, several British columns from various directions, commanded by Havelock, Campbell and Outram, and Gurkha soldiers led by Jung Bahadur advanced towards Lucknow to rescue the people confined in the Residency. But Indian fighters kept them at bay for several months. At last, the enemy began to close in on the city. The siege of Lucknow Residency lasted from 25th May to 27th November 1857.

The last of the rebels left Lucknow on 21st March 1858, when the British succeeded in wresting it from the Begum's soldiers, recapturing the residency, along with the city of Lucknow.

Begum's soldiers fought tenaciously, resisting till the last. They fought the British on the streets of Lucknow, meeting bullets and cannons with spears, swords and lathis. Riding an elephant, the Begum directed her fighters on the battlefield but she finally lost the city to the British. Maulvi Ahmadullah Shah and the chiefs who had helped her

scattered into groups to continue the fight. Refusing to surrender, she was finally forced to flee to Nepal.

Maulvi Ahmadullah Shah and the chiefs who had helped her scattered into groups to continue the fight. However, he was soon killed at Shahjahanpur. Pleased with the win, the British displayed his head at their office as a victory trophy. Other chiefs like Rana Beni Madho, Maharaja Gulab Singh and Narpat Singh also fought relentlessly before being defeated.

NANA SAHIB OF BITHUR

Nana Sahib was the adopted son of Baji Rao II, the last of the Maratha rulers. Baji Rao had been sent to live at Bithur, near Kanpur, after he was defeated in the last Maratha War. When Baji Rao died, the English refused to pay pension to his adopted son, in spite of an agreement signed by the British promising the same. Nana Dhanaji Rao, popularly known as Nana Sahib, decided to fight for his rights. He sent Azimullah Khan, his trusted agent, to England to plead his case. The authorities turned a deaf ear, and Azimullah returned empty-handed. It is believed that the two started plotting the war against the foreigners only after losing faith in the law. Nana travelled extensively during this period along with another rebel leader Tantia Tonpe. Since everything was carried out in great secrecy, several details about this incident are still unknown.

As fighting spread across the region, Nana Sahib, who was friendly with the English in Kanpur, offered to look after their treasury. But when the revolt began, he joined the soldiers' cause.

The British, under General Wheeler, took shelter in a small building. The Indian rebels soon surrounded the British, and after a siege lasting three weeks took their revenge by killing all the Englishmen. Nana Sahib then declared himself as the Peshwa.

When fresh British troops arrived under Havelock, he fought them on the banks of River Pandu. Defeated, he retreated only to fight once again on the Grand Trunk Road. He fought a brilliant battle but lost to the colonizer. Undaunted, he rallied more men around him and returned to battle again and again. The superior force of the British defeated Nana Sahib, who was forced to cross the Ganges and retreat to Nepal. At Banki on the river Rapti, Nana Sahib, along with the Begum of Awadh and other leaders, made a resolve. Though defeated, they would not surrender. Nana Sahib chose to ride off into the jungles of Nepal. Defiant to the last, he questioned the British in these words:

Diamond feather worn by Peshwa rulers on their turbans

> "What right have you to occupy India and declare me an outlaw? Who gave you (the) right to rule over India? What, you *firangis*, the king? And we (are) thieves in our own country?"
> Nana Sahib

TANTIA TONPE

The battle was carried on by Nana's General and loyal follower Tantia Tonpe. He fought several battles against the British Army across Awadh and Central India, along with Nana's nephew, Rao Sahib. When he was at a place called Kalpi, he received an urgent call from Rani of Jhansi for help. Accompanied by several other chiefs, he rushed to the spot and had a fierce encounter with Sir Hugh Rose, who forced him to retreat to Kalpi. The Rani was able to join him and the two succeeded in capturing the Fort at Gwalior. Even though faced by the British on both sides, they fought the rulers till their last breath. Tonpe, who was being pursued relentlessly by four detachments of enemy troops, managed to flee with his men.

Tonpe was shrewd enough to realize he would never be able to match the superior strength of the enemy. This is why he started the clever game of guerilla warfare. With lightning swiftness, he moved from place to place. Appearing from nowhere, he swooped down on the enemy, routing their troops. When defeat faced him, he slipped from their grasp, only to mobilize his forces to attack again. For ten long months, the British forces were kept busy chasing this wily warrior. Across Central India into Rajputana, backward and forwards, the British were forced to follow him until Tonpe at last hid himself in the jungles of the Chambal. If not for a friend who betrayed him by disclosing his hiding place to the British, Tonpe might have remained uncaught. Nabbed by the British while he was asleep, Tonpe was given a death sentence. He walked up to the gallows, with his head held high, proud and defiant till the end.

An equestrian statue of Laxmibai, in Solapur, Maharashtra, where she is seen charging into battle with her little son, Damodar, on her back.

THE GALLANT QUEEN OF JHANSI

1854 British Issue Gazette Dissolving Jhansi
• **1858** British Begin Siege of Jhansi • **1858** British Troops
Advance to Kotah ki Serai

The 1857 War gave rise to several military leaders. They were people of grit and courage who took up a difficult challenge and fought against tremendous odds. The bravest and most brilliant of these warriors was none other than Rani Laxmibai of Jhansi.

The countless stories, ballads and poems inspired by this courageous queen are a testimony of her matchless bravado. The pages of history fully justify the praises showered on this legendary soldier queen.

An English lawyer, John Lang, employed by the Rani, described her in the following words:

Rani Laxmibai and Gangadhar Rao

"Her face must have been very handsome when she was younger, and even now it had many charms. The expression was very good and intelligent. The eyes were particularly fine, and the nose very delicately shaped."

John Lang, an English lawyer

Laxmibai was the daughter of Moropant Tambe of Benares. Her real name was Manikarnika. Tampe later moved to the court of Baji Rao II at Bithur, near Kanpur. Affectionately called Manu, Laxmibai showed great interest in activities like horse-riding, sword-fighting and other martial arts.

When she was still a child, Laxmibai was married to Gangadhar Rao of Jhansi. The State of Jhansi was then a small Maratha principality in the heart of Bundelkhand in Central India. Her husband's family gave Manu the name Laxmibai.

THE DOCTRINE OF LAPSE

Gangadhar Rao was much older than his wife. The couple had a son who died when he was a few months old. Soon after, Gangadhar Rao also fell ill, but a day before his death he adopted a boy from another branch of his family. He did this in the presence of not only nobles of his court, but also a British officer-in-charge named Major Ellis. Rao handed over a letter to the government, informing them of the adoption and announcing that Jhansi would henceforth be looked after by his wife Laxmibai on behalf of their adopted son, Damodar Rao.

The letter was duly received in Calcutta by Governor-General Lord Dalhousie, who could not have cared less about its contents. For him it was only an opportunity to seize the State of Jhansi under the policy of "Doctrine of Lapse". A letter, dated 7th March 1854, dissolving the State of Jhansi, was sent to Major Ellis by the British government to convey the message to the Queen of Jhansi.

When Laxmibai heard that her state had been annexed, she declared angrily, "I will not give up my Jhansi!" However, realizing she had no other alternative at that moment, she kept quiet and bided her time.

But the loss of Jhansi rankled in the proud queen's heart.

The doctrine of lapse was a policy of annexation initiated by the East India Company and brought in by Lord Dalhousie. Under this policy, if any ruler of a princely state, which comes under the control of East India Company, died without any legal heir, that particular state would be annexed by the Company. Also, any adopted heir could not proclaim any right to the kingdom but only inherit the personal properties of the king. This ultimately took away the long-held authority of a king to appoint his legal heir.

It is said that she, along with Tantia Tonpe and Nana Sahib, made secret plans to wage war against foreign rule.

Later, before the 1857 revolt spread to Bundelkhand, Jhansi remained surprisingly silent. The British officers posted in Jhansi were led to believe that the Rani would remain their faithful ally.

In June 1857, Laxmibai's soldiers shot dead British officers stationed at the Jhansi Fort. They declared Laxmibai as the Queen of Jhansi and rode off to join their comrades in Delhi. Soon, Laxmibai began to look after the affairs of the state on behalf of her son.

Assuming that a woman would be ill-equipped to defend her kingdom, enemies like Sadashiv Rao, who was a relative of Laxmibai and the ruler of Orchha, a neighbouring state, tried to take control of Jhansi. Laxmibai showed him she was no weakling. By defeating the Orchha ruler and others roundly, she sent out a clear message that she could not be taken lightly.

Even after defeating these enemies, Laxmibai knew she could not sit idle. Soon she would have to face a mightier foe. She began to prepare for the battle with the British. She strengthened the defences of the Fort of Jhansi, inspected the grounds around the ramparts and chalked out her strategy. She also trained women in horse-riding and shooting. She stocked up ammunition and set up a powder factory inside the Fort. The Queen also wrote to her allies, the Rajas of Banpur, Shahgarh and other Bundela chiefs, besides Tantiya Tonpe, to help her in her fight. As a result of her vigorous efforts, Jhansi became a strong state, well-organized and ready for war.

Sir Hugh Rose, as Commander of the Central India Field Force, soon marched closer and closer to Jhansi. He arrived in Jhansi on 21st March 1858. Rose was joined by Brigadier General Stuart who had just captured the Fort of Chanderi. If these two stalwarts of the British Army imagined that Laxmibai would be frightened into surrendering, they were in for a shock. The news of the arrival of the British troops at the doorstep of the Fort did not sway her determination.

Inside the Fort, the Rani prepared feverishly to meet the challenge. Wearing a male attire, she galloped from rampart to rampart, inspecting, giving quick, sharp orders to her gunners, instructing women responsible for supplying the ammunition and provisions. The British soon began firing. In return, Rani's soldiers also fired continuous shots from the Fort. Riding a white horse amidst these bullets and cannonballs, Laxmibai remained at the forefront, inspiring people with her courage. The fierce fighting continued for seven days. Several times the walls of the Fort were breached, but to the surprise of British officers, they were repaired miraculously by dawn. Under their Queen's guidance, the gunners worked such wonders that even the enemy forces were left impressed.

WITH A LITTLE HELP FROM FRIENDS

On the 7th day, the powder factory in the tamarind grove was destroyed by a cannonball, as its location was disclosed by a treacherous insider. Thirty-eight men and women were killed. The wall of the fort was also badly breached. The enemy was about to advance into the Fort. Fortunately, news came in of the arrival of Tantia Tonpe along with his large force. It gave a new hope to the besieged soldiers inside the Fort.

Sir Hugh decided to drive off the rescue party. Leaving a portion of his force in Jhansi, he advanced towards Tonpe. His attack was successful and Tonpe was forced to retreat towards Kalpi. A triumphant Hugh returned to his attack of Jhansi.

Meanwhile, Laxmibai rallied her disheartened troops and urged them to fight on. "Jhansi looks to nobody for help," she told her sirdars, "you fight not for your lives, but for your honour and honour lies in death. Long after you are dead, bards will sing your praises and homes in India will light lamps in your memory. Die then the death of heroes."

When Sir Hugh attempted to re-enter Jhansi, a sharp hail of bullets greeted him. Various types of missiles were now hurled at the enemy such as earthen pots filled with gunpowder, logs of wood, rocks and boulders. At last, a gate gave way. Enemy soldiers tried to rush in, but huge rocks and boulders blocked their way. The heavy barrage let loose on them forced them to retreat with several casualties. They tried to climb the ramparts and managed to breach the wall again.

The entry of British sepoys was no signal for the battle to stop. Laxmibai and her men were determined to resist. The battle went on for days on each and every street of Jhansi till the last man was felled. Women chose to jump into wells rather than fall into the hands of the enemy. A terrible loot and plunder of the city followed. The British snatched away jewellery from people and robbed the city of all its riches. The library containing ancient and precious manuscripts was not spared either. It was set on fire by the vengeful British soldiers.

At last, the brave Queen's courage wavered as she shed tears to see the destruction of these valuable and ancient treasures. Vowing to take revenge, she boldly escaped through the north gates of the Fort, followed by her loyal Pathan soldiers.

She knew the area well and galloped off towards Kalpi. Her son Damodar, for whose sake she fought so bravely, clung to her back, tied with a silken scarf.

When Sir Hugh discovered that his enemy had slipped away, he quickly dispatched his officers to chase and capture the Queen. After a hot pursuit, Lieutenant Dowker of the 14th Light Dragoons began to gain ground. Laxmibai felled him with one swipe of her sword and soon left her pursuers far behind. Galloping all through the dead of night and under a hot sun the next day, she reached Kalpi at midnight. Here she was welcomed by Tantia Tonpe and Rao Sahib.

The three fought together at Koonch and Kalpi but since the troops under Laxmibai were no longer the organized force that had served the Queen well in Jhansi, the fighters were defeated. However, their spirits remained high and they decided to meet at a place called Gopalpur to make fresh plans. It was Laxmibai's brilliant idea to seize the fort at Gwalior. The ruler of Gwalior, Jayajirao Scindia, supported the British by giving them access. Laxmibai knew that if the fort was captured, the British would be cut off from the west and their supply line would be broken. It would also provide the Indian leaders with a good control over the south.

Tonpe succeeded in getting the soldiers of Scindia over to his side. As the three warriors closed in on Gwalior, Scindia opened fire on them. His soldiers, however, rushed to join his enemies. After his fort was captured by Laxmibai and her allies, Scindia fled to Agra to save his life. The vast store of ammunition found at Gwalior replenished their stock and helped Tonpe and his allies carry on the fight. Rao Sahib was declared the Peshwa on behalf of his uncle, Nana Sahib, and the occasion was celebrated with great joy. However, Laxmibai did not waste any time celebrating the win and started preparations for the next challenge. She knew the British would soon strike Gwalior.

The seizure of Gwalior came as a great shock to the English. With determined vigour, they marched to re-capture this strategic spot. Rao Sahib turned to Laxmibai for advice on how to meet the challenge. It was decided that the Queen would defend Gwalior on the eastern side. Facing her was Brigadier Smith. War bugles blew on the morning of 17th June 1858, as British troops advanced from Kotah-ki-Serai towards the hills, which were being defended by the Queen. The British suffered heavy casualties on the first day as repeated and fierce attacks were made by the rebel forces.

Early next morning, clad in male attire, wearing a pearl necklace and covered in steel armour, Laxmibai sat astride a white horse before her troops. She was followed by two of her loyal warriors, Mundar and Kashi Bai. Once again, the fearless Queen led fierce attacks on enemy troops. Though the men surrounding her fell one by one, she continued to fight, thrusting her sword left and right. Soon she was left with just a few sirdars.

When Mundar screamed and fell, Laxmibai rushed to her aid. She killed the soldier responsible for the death of her friend. About to cross a drain, Laxmibai's horse stumbled. Just then, she was hit by a bullet. Soon after, a sword struck her face and shoulder. At last, this brave and courageous woman, who fought her enemies till the end, fell, to rise no more.

Sir Hugh Rose, her sworn enemy who had attacked and relentlessly pursued her— from Jhansi to Koonch and Kalpi, and finally to Gwalior, paid his fair enemy a glorious tribute when he called her "the best and bravest military leader of the rebels".

Inspired by her valiant deeds, renowned poetess Subhadra Kumari Chauhan wrote these famous lines in Hindi:

जाओ रानी याद रखेंगे ये कृतज्ञ भारतवासी,
यह तेरा बलिदान जगावेगा स्वतंत्रता अविनसी,
होवे चुप इतिहास, लगे सच्चाई को चाहे फाँसी,
हो मदमाती विजय, मिटा दे गोलों से चाहे झाँसी ।

तेरा स्मारक तू ही होगी, तू खुद अमिट निशानी थी,
बुंदेले हरबोलों के मुँह हमने सुनी कहानी थी,
खूब लडी मर्दानी वह तो झाँसी वाली रानी थी ॥

The siege of Arrah, which took place during the Great Indian Uprising, was the eight-day defence of a fortified outbuilding by British sepoys against the forces of Kunwar Singh.

THE BRAVE BUT FAILED REVOLTS

1857 Siege of Arrah • **1857** Kunwar Singh's Army Surrounds the
Billiard Room at Arrah • **1858** Death of Kunwar Singh

While Laxmibai faced her adversaries in Central India, another leader, Kunwar Singh of Jagdishpur, carried on a spirited struggle in the eastern state of Bihar.

Patna, the capital of Bihar, was at one time a stronghold of the Wahabis, the followers of Syed Ahmad, who had given the British a difficult time before the 1857 uprising. The Magistrate of Patna, William Taylor, therefore, took extra precautions once the revolt started in Delhi. When, in spite of this a riot broke out in Patna, he caught and hanged the culprits, all twenty-four of them. Indian soldiers, full of fury, later fired at their officers and marched towards Arrah.

A few miles away from Arrah lived Kunwar Singh, the ruler of Jagdishpur. These soldiers placed themselves under his leadership. The chief had his own reasons to join the war and readily agreed. The eighty-year-old Rajput displayed extraordinary feats of valour and military skill. He proved to be more energetic, aggressive and spirited than many other younger men.

SIEGE OF ARRAH

On 27th July 1857, Kunwar Singh's men surrounded the small billiard room at Arrah where British officers had taken shelter. An officer called Captain Dunbar was hastily dispatched from Patna to rescue the British.

Dunbar's troops reached the outskirts of Arrah at night. After reaching the town, the British forces received information that the rebel troops had fled after hearing news of his arrival. Relieved, Dunbar and his men casually marched through a thick grove of mango trees. They had no idea it was a trick played by the clever enemy to trap their troops.

It was pitch-dark under the trees. Suddenly, a hail of bullets struck the unwary British troops. Every tree seemed to emit fire. Kunwar Singh's men, hidden behind trees and bushes, fired from all directions, even from treetops. Kunwar Singh and his team

Eighty-year-old Kunwar Singh,
more energetic, aggressive and
spirited than many a younger man

chased the fleeing English soldiers, until only a handful of the 450 men were left to tell the tragic tale.

Out of these, a few escaped and took refuge in Arrah House. These men were rescued by the British army, forcing Kunwar Singh to retreat. His palace was captured by the British but the brave commander did not give up.

He moved with his followers, including women and children, into the jungles near the banks of the River Sone. He marched westwards towards Central India. Wherever he went, local chiefs, soldiers and civilians flocked to fight under his banner. At Kanpur, he was joined by Tantia Tonpe. When he learnt that English and Nepalese troops were marching from Azamgarh towards Awadh to help British troops in Lucknow, he decided to return east to fight them in Azamgarh.

Kunwar Singh was old and experienced. He had the pragmatism to realize, like Tantia Tonpe, that it was impossible to match the British with their vast resources of organized manpower. The only way out was to resort to guerilla tactics, using his wit and intelligence against British might and power.

Kunwar Singh's troops encamped near Atraulia, near Azamgarh. When Colonel Milman attacked the rebel troops, they retreated to the Fort, pretending defeat. As soon as Milman took a break to relax with his men and sit down for breakfast, bullets began to rain down on them. Kunwar Singh's soldiers, who were waiting for an opportune moment, swooped down on the British forces. Poor Milman was forced to flee, chased by Kunwar Singh. Milman somehow reached another camp under an officer called Dames, who was furious to hear of the trick and vowed to destroy the Indian chief.

But it was Kunwar Singh who forced Dames and Milman to flee. He chased them until they were forced to take refuge in a fort at Azamgarh.

The British government was alarmed when news of these shameful defeats reached them. Troops were immediately dispatched from Calcutta, Benares and Lucknow to subdue this new menace. But Kunwar Singh managed to crush the troops, which were this time led by an officer called Lord Kerr. Encouraged by his numerous victories, he left for Jagdishpur, with the aim of hoisting his own flag once again atop his palace. On the way, he had to cross the river Ganga. He knew the enemy would lie there in wait. To outsmart the British, Kunwar Singh spread the rumour that his troops would cross a certain spot atop elephants. The English hid themselves around this spot. But the shrewd ruler eluded them yet again. His men crossed quietly on boats a few miles away. When the English general learnt of this, he rushed his troops to the spot. The last of the boats was crossing the river. The British managed to spot Kunwar Singh and opened fire. One of the bullets hit his arm. With one swipe of his heavy sword, the fearless warrior cut off his arm at the elbow and threw it into the river. "I offer this to you, Mother Ganga!" he said as he made this sacrifice.

Kunwar Singh cutting off his arm

Describing the British defeat in Arrah, an English eyewitness wrote,

"Forces of Kunwar Singh closed on our disgrace and the disaster was complete... Orders were thrown to the winds. Discipline and drill were dead... all was confusion and terror."

Kunwar Singh won back his home. Once again, he reigned supreme in Jagdishpur. Unfortunately, he could not enjoy his victory for long. The wrist injury soon turned fatal and led to the death of this heroic old man.

The fight was carried on by his brother, Amar Singh, who also relied on guerrilla warfare to combat the British forces until he was forced to flee to the jungles.

By the end of 1858, the East India Company had put down all those who had attempted to fight against them. However, the revolt had been widespread and had continued for years. In Assam, Maniram Dewan and Piyali Barua were at the forefront, while in Orissa, Princes of Sambalpur, Surendra Sahi, Ujjal Sahi and Dandasena took the lead. Northern India was represented by Awadh, Rohilkhand, Bundelkhand, Allahabad, Agra and Meerut; Bihar by Kunwar Singh and his brother, and the Maulvis of Sadikpur, Rajgir, Amarthu, etc. In the United Provinces (now called Uttar Pradesh), there was not a village that was not represented. There were uprisings at some places in Punjab, though they were crushed by the British. The main centres of disturbance in Rajasthan were Kotah and Auwa, a dependency of Jodhpur princely state.

Central India was very much a part of the struggle. In the Deccan and Southern part of India, there were centres of revolt but the resistance did not spread as widely as in other parts of the country. Rebels were active in Madras, in the territories of Hyderabad and Malabar. There were countless heroes of war who became martyrs for the cause of freedom. The chiefs, zamindars and princes who had led the war were put down by the end of 1858. Some had been killed, others arrested and hanged to death or forced to flee to the jungles.

END OF THE BLOODY WAR

Like most wars, the 1857 First War of Independence was marked by violence and bloodshed. The Indian soldiers, fed up with British oppression, began by killing and shooting their foreign officers. The British retaliated by wreaking terrible vengeance on the rebels. Innocent citizens were massacred at will, homes looted and destroyed, and whole villages set on fire, to teach the people a lesson they would never forget. Soldiers were tied to cannons, to be blown to bits by merciless British forces.

People were hung to death from branches of trees. An officer called Neil even strung bodies on roadside trees while marching towards Kanpur. On the one hand, the British accused Nana Sahib of cruelty for killing British officers, on the other, the British were killing a hundred thousand times more and even boasted of their cruel deeds.

Even as both British and rebel forces indulged in large-scale looting and plunder, there were soul-stirring deeds of courage, valour and heroic resistance on either side. All these acts of rebellion were an inspiration for future acts of defiance. The wars fought by the Queen of Jhansi, Tantia Tonpe and many others are also remembered for bravery of the highest order.

BAHADUR SHAH ZAFAR

The great uprising of 1857 was also marked by large-scale participation of the civilian population including artisans from cities and peasants and farmers from the villages. Hindus and Muslims battled side by side under the leadership of the Emperor of Delhi, Bahadur Shah Zafar, who was acknowledged as the head by leaders of both religions. They fought for a common cause – to get rid of the oppressive regime. The British termed the uprising a "mutiny" or rebellion of sepoys. However, considering the scale of involvement of all sections of society extending to almost the whole of India for a common cause, the war came to be regarded as India's First War of Independence.

What set the war apart was that for the first time several rulers and kings had fought together.

In spite of the heroic spirit, Indians could not defeat the British. There were several reasons for this.

Bahadur Shah Zafar, the emperor of Delhi

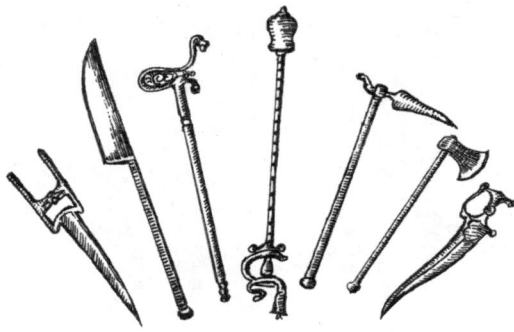

not defeat the British. There were several reasons for this.

Being a strong imperial force with colonies spread all over Africa, China and Australia, the British could draw support from across the seas. Troops poured into India to crush the revolt. The British were also better organized. Their troops maintained a high degree of discipline and their planning was done centrally by one single authority. Also, while the Indians fought with outdated weapons such as swords, spears, guns and muskets captured from the British, the enemy was well-equipped with the latest weapons of war. The recently-introduced telegraph services also provided the British with faster means of communication.

But the most important reason for this failure was the lack of unity amongst the Indian chiefs. If they had displayed a sense of solidarity and fought together as one unit, the course of history might have taken a different turn. The Indian soldiers remained divided, some being loyal to their British masters. Several of the feudal lords also gave their support to the foreign ruler and backed them wholeheartedly. Besides, many Indian rulers plotted against each other for selfish reasons and could not put up a united front.

In contrast to the British who fought under a supreme authority with great nationalistic zeal and patriotic spirit, India was a country divided. Several big and small states under different feudalistic rulers made up the geographical entity that was India. It was only natural that each kingdom would serve its own interests.

India had not yet emerged as a nation.

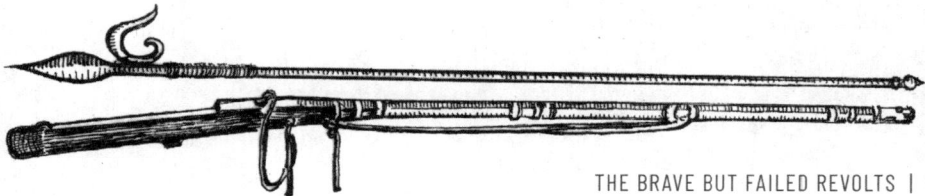

The 1857 War was to be the end of the East India Company. The British government effectively abolished the Company in 1858, handing over the Indian affairs to the British Crown.

MAKERS OF
THE NATION

1828 Raja Rammohan Roy Sets Up Brahmo Samaj • **1858** Transfer of Power from East India Company to the British Monarchy • **1866** Famine in Orissa • **1878** Vernacular Press Act

The countrywide response to the 1857 War shook the British. They realized just how delicate was foundation on which the Empire rested. The rich treasure house, which they had fleeced with such impunity, had been almost lost to them. With the aim of curbing the possibility of a repeat of such an uprising, they announced several changes in the administration.

BRITISH CROWN TAKES OVER

A proclamation was issued by Queen Victoria on 1st November 1858. From the hands of the East India Company, the country was passed on to the Crown, that is under the direct rule of the British government in England. An officer was appointed to look after the Indian affairs. Army discipline was tightened further. The government also promised not to expand its territory further. It tried to appease the princes of the States, chiefs and landowners by promising them special favours on the condition that they remained loyal. With the coming together of these different states and principalities under one administrative head, India became one country.

To further develop trade and commerce and to increase their profits from the colony, the British aimed to reach all parts of the country. They laid a wide network of railways across the length and breadth of India. The arrival of postal and telegraph services made communication quicker, connecting the country like never before.

However, the expansion and ambitious plans of the British led to one significant change. The government now wanted to educate Indians so as to use their services in running the country. Educated men were needed to man the posts and railways. The government, therefore, allowed Christian

missionaries to open schools in towns. In 1857, universities were opened in Madras, Calcutta and Bombay for higher education. The emerging middle class in India consisting of traders, small landholders and merchants took advantage of the new education infrastructure. The knowledge of English helped in their professional advancement. More importantly, it succeeded in connecting various regions like Bengal, Punjab, Kerala, and others through the use of a common language.

Administration through one ruler, quicker and easier flow of communication, and a common language made India one physical and geographical entity.

However, the changes that blew across the Indian Subcontinent left an indelible mark on the Indian economy. Before the arrival of the British, Mughal rule had not brought any fundamental change in the economic structure of India. The economic model of the country was still based on the traditional concept of a self-sufficient village. The Mughals made great progress in trade but did not rely on imports and largely remained self-sufficient.

In sharp contrast, the British conquerors exploited Indian resources and disrupted the traditional economy.

With the coming of the railways, which connected far-flung villages, British goods could be distributed to the remotest areas. Cottage industries like cotton weaving, silk and woollen textiles, iron, pottery, glasswork, paper, metals, tanning and dyeing were swept aside. The poor artisans and craftsmen were forced to abandon their ancestral trades and look for an alternative means of livelihood. With the gradual decline and removal of Indian rulers, the royal patronage to Indian arts and handicrafts also declined, leaving the artisans jobless and poor.

Meanwhile, England had made good progress. Advancement of scientific ideas had led to new inventions and brought in the use of machines. Factories and industries sprung up around the cities to manufacture various goods. Agriculture had given way to industry. India and other colonies of the British Empire added to the Crown's wealth by constantly providing raw material to run the factories in England.

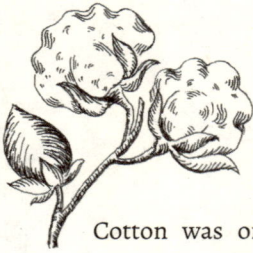

Cotton was one such raw material. For centuries, India had been the largest exporter of cotton textiles in the world. By imposing a high duty on cotton imports to Britain and the rest of Europe, the British succeeded in discouraging the export of Indian cotton textiles. Having lost its markets, India was compelled to sell raw cotton and import textiles from Britain.

THE ECONOMIC DRAIN

Over centuries, Indian craftsmen had perfected the art of cotton weaving which was admired the world over. Before the arrival of the British, a flourishing textile industry had existed in Indian towns, which provided employment to thousands of weavers, dyers and printers. The "mulmul" produced by Indian artisans was so fine that it could easily pass through a small ring.

After the arrival of the British, foreign traders started to ship raw cotton from India to factories in Lancashire and Manchester in Britain, where it was spun into mill-made cloth. Weavers and artisans in India were now without work. To make sure there was no room for any competition with Indian products, British traders even went to the extent of chopping off the hands of skilled workers.

Other raw materials like silk, wool, silver and iron were also sent to England to be manufactured into goods which were brought back to India and sold at high rates. Thus, the British gains from their colonies were two-fold. No wonder then the British policy did not allow the growth of Indian industry, which could have sustained the local craftsmen.

Left without jobs, the artisans returned to their villages. From 1858-1905, more than 90% of the country's population lived in villages. The rural land resources could not support the massive population. As a result, there were terrible famines in the country. In the fifty years between 1860 and 1908, twenty were considered famine years. Major famines in Orissa and Bengal (1866), Rajasthan (1868), Madras (1876), Punjab

(1899) and Kashmir (1878) killed thousands of Indians.

The British revenue collection policies also caused great misery. Land revenue was extorted in different ways. In the zamindari system, a middleman collected rent from the cultivator in the form of grain or cash. Keeping a part as commission, the zamindar would pay the rest to the government. In states like Bengal, Bihar and Orissa, the land revenue was fixed as a certain permanent amount. The rates were not very high, but since it was a permanent settlement, the middlemen or zamindars began to consider the land as their own property and the cultivators were reduced to tenants, who were at the mercy of these landlords. In other parts of India such as Awadh, the revenue rates were revised from time to time. These areas came under the temporary zamindari settlement.

Under the Ryotwari settlement, which prevailed in Bombay and Madras, the government dealt directly with the cultivator who was considered the owner of the land. The rent fixed was exorbitant in this case. The cultivator was often left to starve since the government could increase the tax as and when it wanted to. The high revenue had to be paid irrespective of the agricultural output.

Whatever the system, the fact remained that the old land revenue model was destroyed by the British. Land could now be sold or mortgaged. To pay the high revenue imposed by the British, people began to borrow from money lenders and fell into debt. Unable to pay arrears, landowners had to put up their land for sale. Thus, the peasant lost his land to the British. As a result, misery and despair ailed the country.

"Under the British Indian despot the man is at peace, there is no violence; his substance is drained away, unseen, peaceably and subtly – he starves in peace, and perishes in peace, with law and order."
Dadabhai Naoroji

The anger of impoverished, starving farmers and peasants was bound to explode one day. The 1857 revolt was marked by large-scale participation of peasants. There had been reports of peasants targeting zamindars in Madras, Gujarat, Bengal and Bihar.

The greatest of these peasant revolts was the Indigo agitation in Bengal in 1880. Indigo, grown in Bengal and Bihar for the beautiful dye its plant produced, brought in good profits. The British merchants forced farmers to cultivate the plant and paid them low prices in return. Hungry farmers who were desperate to switch over to other crops were beaten and imprisoned. At last, the peasants rose in defiance in 1859. They attacked government offices and the homes of exploitative indigo traders.

The rebellion attracted the attention of the educated class inspiring writers such as Bengali author Dinabandhu Mitra to write a play called *Nil Darpan*, which described the sufferings of the indigo farmers. The picture of misery painted by Mitra moved people so much that they could not help but join in the peasants' cause. Many educated Indians wrote letters in newspapers and organized meetings to protest against the exploitation.

Similar movements had taken place in the past, when peasants in Poona and Malabar rose against exploitation at the hands of the British.

However, all this had no effect on the insensitive British government.

THE NEW EDUCATED CLASS

Things seemed to be changing. The peasants now had the sympathy and support of the new educated middle class which was emerging in the big cities as a result of English education. This new educated class replaced the chiefs, royal rulers, Brahmin priests and nawabs of the old feudal system, and consisted of traders, moneylenders, lawyers, clerks, officers working in the administration and other professionals.

The British had established their education system with the aim of teaching Indians to think and behave like the English, so that they could be used to serve them better.

The spread of Western ideas through English medium schools and colleges, and foreign books and newspapers led to a feeling of inferiority among educated Indians. The British believed that it was their duty as a superior race to bring culture and civilization to Indians, whom they considered as an "inferior race". The English poured ridicule on Indians and their ways. However, India had once been a rich cultural land having spiritual excellence. Due to centuries of misrule, its rich traditional character got diluted, resulting in rigid and regressive practices such as sati and child marriage.

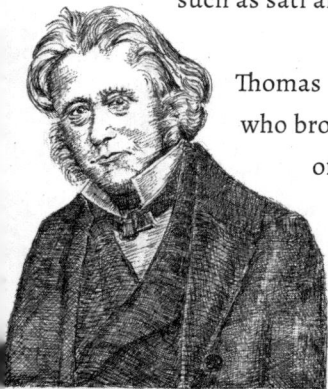

Thomas Babington Macaulay

Thomas Babington Macaulay, who brought in the new system of education, once said, "Indians were a race debased by 3000 years of despotism and priesthood and sunk in slavery and superstition".

Fresh ideas from the West forced Indians to re-examine their beliefs and values in light of the new scientific outlook they had gained.

The Indian educated class was greatly influenced by the ideas of freedom and equality through revolutions in France, America and other countries.

Americans had fought for Independence in the 18th century. The American Declaration of Independence states, "All men are created equal, that they are endowed by their creator with certain rights; that among these rights are life, liberty and the pursuit of happiness".

As a result of these ideas of freedom and equality, Indian reformers also tried to reform the society by removing the prevailing inequality and oppression. It paved the way for a new kind of Indian which replaced the sense of inferiority. By delving into India's past and re-discovering her glorious heritage, these religious and social reformers succeeded in restoring a sense of pride in the Indians. They united the country by re-discovering the idea of the Oneness of Spirit, which forms the basic essence of all religions.

Raja Rammohan Roy was the earliest of these thinkers. Born in Bengal in 1774, he can be called the morning star of a new dawn in Indian thinking, for he set fresh trends in Indian culture by his ideas of religious reform. Roy dug into the origins of our own culture to gain a better understanding of Indian thought. He also studied Western religion and philosophy and advocated a synthesis of all that was valuable in both Indian and Western philosophy. As a learned scholar of several languages like Sanskrit, Persian, Arabic, English, French, Latin, Greek and Hebrew, he read several books and learnt about different religions.

He tried to rid Hindu society of its unjust social customs. The social reformer fought all his life against the practice of sati and aroused public opinion against it. Roy was a champion of women's rights and attacked polygamy and ill treatment of widows. He also spoke in favour of women having a share in inherited property.

In 1828, Roy founded a new religious society called the Brahmo Samaj. Based on Roy's extensive study of the *Vedas* and the *Upanishads*, this religious society preached the worship of one God. It opposed rituals and laid emphasis on the "worship and adoration of the eternal, unsearchable and immutable".

Raja Rammohan Roy

A widow forced to perform Sati

Roy believed that it was important to remove ignorance and the ills of Hindu society before fighting for freedom from the British. He did so by educating the masses through his writings in journals in various languages. Roy died in 1833 at the age of 61 while he was on a visit to Britain.

Maharshi Devendranath (1817-1905) and Keshab Chandra Sen (1838-1884) carried on with the tradition. Keshab Chandra declared, "What we see around us today is a fallen nation, whose primitive greatness lies buried in ruins." He set about trying to revive India's past glory by reminding people of Kalidasa, Shankaracharya, the *Vedas* and the *Upanishads*.

Ishwar Chand Vidyasagar (1820-1891) was a Sanskrit scholar who became the Principal of Sanskrit College. He contributed to the making of modern India in many ways. The most important being his contribution towards the upliftment of women. Vidyasagar led powerful movements for widow remarriage and education for girls. He built many schools for girls and pioneered higher education for women. Vidyasagar also fought against child marriage and polygamy.

Henry Derozio (1809-1832) taught at Hindu College from 1826 to 1831. A man of great intellect and burning love for India, he inspired his students by his fiery speeches and taught them to become rational and liberal. He was one of the first poets to write verses in praise of India as a nation:

Ramakrishna Paramhamsa (1836-1886) was born in a village called Kamarpukur in West Bengal, he re-lit the lamp of spiritual knowledge which had almost got extinguished by the wind of western influence and ridicule. He united the people by preaching that all religions were just different paths to reach the same God, the one Supreme Being. He experienced other faiths like Christianity, Islam and Sikhism, and his life was a story of religion in practice.

Mahadev Govind Ranade (1842-1901) was a brilliant and talented judicial officer who took active interest in all aspects of Indian life. He devoted himself to religion and social reform. He took great pride in his Hindu faith in spite of his western education.

He envisaged India as a great nation proud of its past, marching towards a bright future and inspired with high moral ideals.

"My country! In the days of glory past,

A beauteous halo circled round thy brow,

And worshipped as a deity thou vast, Where is that glory, where that reverence now?"

Henry Derozio, in his poem *To India - My Native Land*, 1828

Born in Gujarat, *Dayananda Saraswati* (1824-1883) was responsible for organizing the Arya Samaj. He tried to unite India by preaching a religion common to all. Dayananda propounded that there was only one God, that all men were equal and that there should be love and charity for all. His message appealed to all classes, and spread over Punjab, U.P. and Rajasthan.

Dayananda had said, "Ideas like sati and idol worship crept into Indian society at a much later stage and had to be removed."

It was Dayananda's Arya Samaj that first gave the call "India for Indians".

A disciple of Ramakrishna Paramhamsa, *Swami Vivekananda* (1863-1902) was twenty when he first met his guru. Vivekananda, named Narendrananth Dutta by his parents, travelled across the world to spread his master's message. People flocked to hear this great orator. Reporting on the Parliament of Religions, *The New York Herald* once wrote, "Vivekananda is undoubtedly the greatest figure in the Parliament of Religions. After hearing him, we feel how foolish it is to send missionaries to this learned nation."

Vivekananda's travel made him realize the tragedy of India, sunk as it was in mental wretchedness and

Swami Vivekananda delivering a speech in Chicago

material squalor. He tried to re-establish the pride of Indians in their own culture and tradition. Vivekananda questioned the superiority of the West. Instead of trying to defend his religion against western criticism, he boldly and proudly proclaimed spiritual superiority and greatness. His passionate and forceful words, which won the admiration of the world, greatly elated his fellow Indians and stirred a feeling of self-pride.

Vivekananda believed in building a strong, brave and dynamic nation. Weakness, cowardice and laziness were feelings he could never tolerate. The injustice and suffering around him made him challenge the educated in these passionate words: "So long as the millions live in hunger and ignorance, I hold every man a traitor, who having been educated at their expense, pays not the least heed to them."

Vivekananda believed in the Yoga of Action and wanted mere contemplation and meditation in religion to be replaced by action.

"As different streams mingle their waters in the ocean, so different paths which men take lead to the Lord."
Vivekananda addressing the Parliament of Religions, in Chicago, 1893

Sir Syed Ahmed Khan (1817-1898): The ruin of the Muslim upper class during the 1857 war had been a traumatic event for the Muslims. This class had enjoyed great influence and power during the Mughal rule and had promoted the glorious heritage of Muslim culture through its royal courts. Suddenly, the entire community became an object of contempt and derision in the eyes of the new rulers. There was mutual distrust and hostility between the British and the Muslims. Christian missionaries criticized Islam. It became necessary to reinterpret religion on modern lines to restore the self-respect of the Muslims. Sir Syed took upon himself the task of social reform and education.

Khan would tell his followers that the soul could not be comprehended by ordinary human beings, who needed the Prophet, the perfect one, to interpret the message of God. He believed that the essential principles of the laws of Islam were the same as the laws of nature, and therefore the differences between religions were only superficial and not real.

The liberal ideas of Syed Ahmad Khan had a great impact on Hindu-Muslim unity.

wisdom of its philosophers and saints, they instilled in Indians a sense of pride. The seeds of doubt which were sown by the British during their rule were removed; a new self-confidence emerged in people's hearts.

These feelings were also reflected in the literature of the period. Bankim Chandra

"We both breathe the air of India and take the water of the holy Ganges and the Jamuna. We both consume the products of the Indian soil. We are living and dying together. By living so long in India, the blood of both have changed. The colour of both have become similar. The faces of both, having changed, have become similar."

Syed Ahmad Khan during a meeting at Patna in 1883

Khan prepared a new scheme for Muslim education, and opened the Muhammadan Anglo-Oriental Collegiate School, in 1875, which later became the Aligarh Muslim University and developed into a centre of learning for higher education.

These thinkers were thus the predecessors of the political reformers who later led Indians towards freedom. By placing the focus back on India's past glory and the

Chatterjee (1838-1894) introduced readers to the beautiful phrase "Vande Mataram" in his play *Anand Math* and made it an anthem for Indians.

In Maharashtra, *Vishnu Shastri Chiplunkar* (1850-1882) guided political thought by writing in the *Kesari*. Other newspapers and journals like *Bombay Darpan*, *Digdarshan* and *Prabhakar* created awareness among the people. In Urdu, writers like Syed Ahmad Khan (1871-1898), Mohammad Hussain Azad (1829-1910) and Altaf Hussain Hali (1837-1914) wrote prose and poems on patriotic themes.

The growth of the Indian press further contributed to awareness that was shaping people's minds. *The Times of India* was born in 1861, *The Pioneer* started in 1865 in Allahabad, and *The Statesman* in 1875 in Calcutta. Among other Indian newspapers were *The Standard* (1877), *Hindoo Patriot* (1853), *Indian Mirror* (1862) and *Amrita Bazar Patrika* (1868). *The Herald* appeared in Uttar Pradesh in 1879.

Newspapers brought out in Indian languages greatly influenced the countrymen. At first, they dealt more with social reforms, but later they began to focus on politics. Prominent among these was the *Anand Bazar Patrika*, which was fearless in expressing its views. Others were *Indu Prakash, Native Opinion,*

Deenbandhu in Marathi, *Kohinoor* and *Akhbar-i-A'am* in Urdu, *Swadesamitram* in Tamil, *Vivek Vardhini* and *Andhra Prakashika* in Telugu.

Not very much later, the government grew suspicious of the popularity of these papers and tried to curb freedom of the Press. On 14th March 1878, the Vernacular Press Act was passed to restrain the Press. Later, due to vehement opposition and on the advice of Lord Ripon, the regressive Act was withdrawn.

By this time, a sense of unity and national consciousness was taking root. The Ilbert Bill controversy united the people further. It made Indians realize that no matter how well educated and modern they might become, they would still be considered inferior by the British imperialists.

THE ILBERT BILL

In 1883, Law Member Sir Courtenay Pergine Ilbert came up with a legislative act which tried to change the part of the Criminal Procedure Code that restricted Indian members from taking British people to court. A raging propaganda was raised against the Bill, which was introduced during Lord Ripon's tenure. The reason was simple: The English did not want to be held accountable by Indians for their deeds. They condemned the Bill strongly.

"It is galling… to my countrymen to have natives placed on a level with themselves…"

An Englishman on the Ilbert Bill

The Bill was modified in the face of this hostility. The English were not prepared to be treated at the same level as Indians.

The humiliation and indignity of being a subject nation was felt once again by Indians. The educated class then began to think of ways to fight the injustice.

Sir Courtenay Ilbert

Over 15,000 soldiers and 400 Indian princes, including the Maharaja of Indore (seen here), took part in the Imperial Durbar, which was held in Delhi in 1877.

POLITICAL AWAKENING

1838 India's First Political Association – The Landholders' Society • **1865** London Indian Society • **1877** Imperial Durbar • **1885** Indian National Congress

The early waves of nationalism, as recounted in the previous chapters, sprung from the religious renaissance spearheaded by scholars such as Paramahamsa, Dayananda Saraswati, Keshab Chandra Sen, Shivnath, Debendranath Tagore and Vivekananda. These great thinkers tried to focus on a scientific outlook to modernize Indian society. The simultaneous spread of English education resulted in the growth of a new middle class. As this class grew, their appetite for money, authority and status also grew. It brought with it greater awareness of the economic drain, exploitation by rulers, and unfairness of the judiciary. Thanks to this evolved thought process, the political awakening of the masses was a possibility.

BIRTH OF POLITICAL THOUGHT

Indians began to establish political associations to represent general grievances against the government. The educated class also started spreading political awareness and initiated discussions in the country.

The first political association of India came into being in 1838. The Landholders Society in Calcutta was aimed at promoting the interests of rich zamindars who employed an army of peasants to work on their land. The association died out by the 1850s. However, just after the First War of Independence, many more such associations took root. Notable among these were the British India Association, Bombay (1851), National Association, Calcutta (1851), and Madras Native Association (1852). These groups agitated on constructive issues and managed to achieve some success in settling matters on a regional basis.

The Indian League, founded by Sisir Kumar Ghosh, in 1875, functioned for a long time in Calcutta. It was succeeded by the Indian National Association (1876) in Bengal, which brought many nationalists like A.O. Hume, Anand Mohan Bose, Surendranath Banerjee, Manmohan Ghose into active politics. These leaders of Bengal laid stress on social, religious and personal freedom.

Surendranath Banerjee

on social, religious and personal freedom. But it was Surendranath Banerjee who focused on political freedom. He believed that every change must be gradual so that the new is "adapted to the old and the old assimilated into the new." His resolute stand on various issues earned him the nickname "Surrender Not" from the Britishers. When Banerjee organized the first National Conference in Calcutta, educationists, professionals and radical thinkers from all over the country gathered together on a common platform for the first time. Banerjee became the first leader to gain countrywide popularity. This great assembly was the precursor of the Indian National Congress.

Soon the spirit of nationalism began to spread to other parts of India. In Maharashtra, the Poona Sarvajanik Sabha (1870) espoused the cause of peasants and asked for some seats to be set aside for Indians in the Parliament. It also demanded that more Indians must be employed in senior positions in the civil service. Its main organizers, Ganesh Vasudev Joshi, Bal Krishna Marathe, Mahadev Govind Ranade and Kashinath Parshuram Gadgil, shared a common cause with British Associations and the India Association. Ranade devoted himself to economic and social upliftment. Being a subordinate judge under the Government of Bombay, he could not take part in politics, but on the basis of his analysis of economic problems, he advocated a policy of industrial and commercial development. Men like Gopal Krishna Gokhale were inspired and got into politics due to Ranade's ideas.

Indian nationalism proved to be a dynamic force that gathered momentum as the years rolled by. These early influences contributed to the nationalist movement. The Madras Native Association (1853) and Madras

Mahajan Sabha (1884) filed a petition, which was signed by 14,000 persons, demanding the termination of the lease of the East India Company. Expectedly, the Governor in Madras took strict measures and suppressed the movement.

As early as 1865, the London Indian Society was established to promote the interests of Indians. Womesh Chunder Bonnerjee, just a law student then, became its Secretary and Dadabhai Naoroji its President. Later, at the initiative of Naoroji, the East India Association (1866), formed in London, spread to different parts of India. Its main function was to voice the problems faced by Indians. Naoroji and Pherozeshah Mehta – both prominent leaders of Bombay – sought reforms from the government,

retaining a sincere faith in British sense of fair play. These leaders relied on the British for their political salvation.

Meanwhile, the Indian intelligentsia became more critical of British policies and probed deeper into the true nature of imperialism. The exploitative nature of British rule also became more evident. Politically conscious people refused to accept that they had to be ruled by Britain forever. Even though the existing political associations at this point were all regional, the resentment against the British policies became widespread. Inevitably, the need of the hour was a pan-India nationalist organization representing the different regions.

INDIAN NATIONAL CONGRESS

At last, in December 1885, the Indian National Congress (INC) was founded with the cooperation of A.O. Hume, a retired English civil servant. Hume was inspired by a genuine feeling of sympathy for the interests and welfare of India.

Though he may not have been fired by the same sense of patriotism as that of Indian leaders, he pleaded hard with Lord Dufferin for the establishment of the Indian National Congress (INC). He appealed for permission for a yearly conference of

Indian politicians, as a friendly gesture from the British government. Bonnerjee became the first President of INC in 1885, which included political thinkers from different parts of the country. Of these, the most prominent were Dadabhai Naoroji, Justice M.G. Ranade, Pherozeshah Mehta, K.T. Telang, Rahimatullah Mohammad Sayani, Vithaldas K. Jhaveri, Uma Shankar Yagnik, V.K. Chilplunkar from Poona; P. Ananda Charlu, A. Subramaniyam Iyer, I. Viraraghavachari from the South. Eastern India was represented by Surendranath Banerjee, Anand Mohan Bose, Lal Mohan Ghose, and Kali Charan Banerjee, all of whom were prominent members of the Indian Association in Calcutta.

The British felt that by allowing a mild political movement, it would be possible to avoid a nationwide resistance. It was for this reason that Governor-General Lord Dufferin suggested to A.O. Hume that the role of the Indian National Congress be limited to social affairs. However, the leaders of INC were aiming towards constitutional reforms and promotion of national interests. The Congress members cooperated with Hume because they did not want to arouse the hostility of the government at the very outset. They also felt that with Hume's support their political conferences would not arouse the suspicions of the British.

Flag of the Indian National Congress

With the foundation of the Indian National Congress, the movement for India's freedom was launched in a small and cautious but organized manner. The leaders were well aware of the subjugation of the poor by the zamindars. These leaders favoured the poor and became their champions. The Congress members would meet from time to time to discuss programmes to educate people about their rights and to arouse a feeling of nationalism among the masses. To create national unity irrespective of class, region and caste was the foremost aim of these programmes.

"Congress," as Nehru wrote later in his letters to his daughter Indira, "took up the cause of the masses and became, to some extent, their champion. It challenged the very basis of British rule in India, and led great mass movements against it."

GRAND OLD MAN OF INDIA

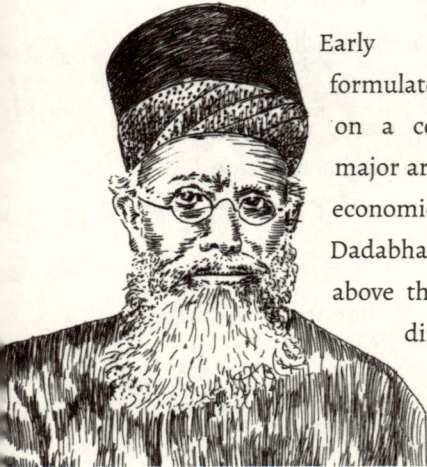

Dadabhai Naoroji

Early Congress leaders formulated their demands on a countrywide basis. A major area of concern was the economic drain of the country. Dadabhai Naoroji towered above the rest in voicing his dissent. He was a man of intellect, reason, pragmatism and generosity. A successful businessman, he dedicated his life and wealth to India's struggle for freedom. Naoroji directed people's attention to the unjust economic policies of the government which aimed to fill the British treasury. India's wealth was being constantly drained

Lovingly called the Grand Old Man of India, Dadabhai Naoroji feverishly wrote articles about the prevailing conditions. He made sure that his write-ups got readership in Europe as well. He made a case for Indians by saying that even though the British were able to maintain law and order in India, the poor were suffering under heavy taxes. These problems could be solved if Indians ruled their own country. Naoroji, for the first time, came up with the idea of Swaraj as the ultimate goal of India.

The INC also objected to India being reduced to a raw material supplier for Britain. Large-scale investments in railways and plantations led to the strengthening of British hold on the Indian economy. The best remedy for economic problems and for removal of poverty was the development of modern industry. The leaders urged the British government to aid Indian industry through subsidies and loans. Besides this, they also demanded technical education for Indians,

particularly in the fields of steel and mining. They also put forth the demand for improving the condition of plantation workers. The existing system of taxation put a heavy burden on the poor, leaving the rich, especially the foreigners, with a lighter load. They demanded scrapping oppressive laws on Salt Tax. Unfortunately in 1888, some of the non-official nominees, mostly zamindars and merchants who toed the official line, supported the increase in Salt Tax.

> Congress made severe attacks on the existing pattern of expenditure which was meant to satisfy the imperial needs of the British.

They condemned the prevailing condition of near starvation among millions in the country. They also protested against the heavy burden on Indian finances on account of the fat salaries being paid to British officers, most of which were sent to Britain. The Indian Civil Services also drained out a large proportion of India's wealth as European civil servants ignored the demands and basic needs of the Indian people. The British policies rendered the most qualified Indian into a permanent state of inferiority in his own country when compared with an Englishman.

Questions were also raised over the tyrannical behaviour of the police. These nationalists demanded the separation of the judiciary from the executive so that people could get some protection from arbitrary acts of the police and bureaucracy. As their civil right, the Congress leaders demanded freedom of speech, thought and association. The Vernacular Press Act of 1878, which sought to gag Indian newspapers, was opposed by the Congress until the British were forced to repeal it. The nationalists gradually moved towards demanding a democratic self-government.

IDEA OF SWADESHI

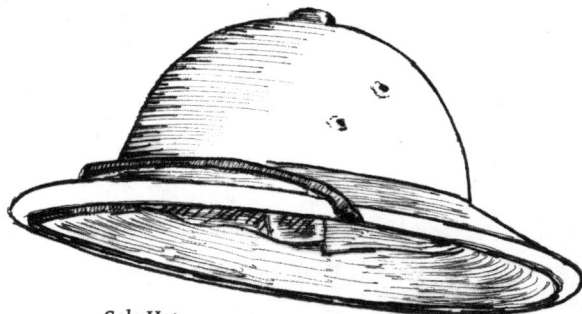

Sola Hat

The economic drain the country was suffering led to the birth of "swadeshi" as a method of protecting Indian industry from the onslaught of British manufacturers. Many swadeshi stores were opened in major cities and towns. A Congress leader and believer in the idea of swadeshi, Ganesh Vasudev Joshi attended the Imperial Durbar in 1877, dressed in khadi. Later in 1896, a powerful swadeshi campaign swept through Maharashtra. Students collected imported cloth, shoes and other items with a foreign trademark and burnt huge bonfires of these foreign goods. The powerful idea of only using swadeshi led to great excitement among students. Many were seen taking off English Sola hats worn by fellow countrymen, as a symbol of boycott.

With each passing year, Congress gained in strength as more and more people joined the cause, including Muslims, who also felt the need to educate their community to promote the ideas of freedom and swadeshi.

THE MODERATES

The moderates were a group of leaders who made appeals for law reforms in a civil and lawful manner and openly expressed their gratitude towards the British when their demands were fulfilled. Their method could be summed up as constitutional agitation – courteous and lawful. The moderates believed that the British were genuinely not aware of the condition of Indians. The quiet brand of politicians were open to dialogue and keen to enlighten both, the British public and the Parliament, through practiced restraint and a mannerly approach in speech and writing.

Of these, Gopal Krishna Gokhale was the foremost

Gopal Krishna Gokhale

leader. Gokhale raised his voice against the British Civil Service, where the most educated Indian was reduced to the status of "Englishman's Labourer". He founded the Servants of India Society (1905), which taught men to devote their lives to the country. With a view to spread patriotic fervour by educating people, he, along with Nam Joshi, Bal Gangadhar Tilak and Gopal Ganesh Agarkar, formed the Deccan Educational Society. All these dedicated men preferred to teach in national schools instead of accepting high posts offered to them by the government. Scholars such as R.P. Paranjpe, a graduate from Cambridge who was given the honour of "Wrangler" (for excellence in mathematics), set a unique example when he accepted the position of the Principal of Ferguson College, at a salary of Rs. 10 per month.

Gopal Krishna Gokhale, who taught economics, appealed to the people to keep the movement peaceful. He feared that the British might crush it completely if the public resorted to violence. A major lesson from the 1857 uprising was that Indians were no match for the British when it came to using military force. The moderates believed that even if the Congress met with initial failures, it would gain strength to accomplish great things in the future.

The Congress grew and propagated the ideas of nationhood. From the very beginning, the British were opposed to the presence of nationalist forces and began to criticize the nationalists as "disloyal babus", "seditious Brahmins" and "violent villains". They had hoped that the National Congress would keep itself busy with social issues and academic discussions. The ruling class described the Congress as a "factory of sedition" for creating political awareness among the public. Coming down heavily on the Indian press, the British deported several editors of nationalistic newspapers on charges of sedition. They sent people to prison and hired spies to shadow

prominent leaders. By 1900, the intention of the British became so obvious that Viceroy Lord Curzon declared it was his ambition to see the death of the Congress.

At this point, the British authorities attempted to create a rift within the people on grounds of caste and religion. They were certain that if differences between Hindus and Muslims and upper-caste and lower-caste Hindus were strengthened, the national movement could be suppressed. The British instigated communal rivalry among educated Indians on the question of jobs in government service. After the 1857 War of Independence, the British had systematically crushed the Muslim upper class by favouring the Hindus. Now they made attempts to turn upper- and middle-class Muslims against the national movement. The divide and rule policy was not confined to Hindu-Muslim differences. Every tactic was played to turn the feudal class against the intelligentsia, caste against caste, group against group and province against province.

Plans were set afoot to exercise greater control on modern liberal education as it inspired rational, democratic and nationalistic ideas.

There was no stopping the rising tide of nationalism. The pioneering work of Dadabhai Naoroji, Surendranath Banerjee and Gopal Krishna Gokhale had succeeded in exposing the true character of British imperialism. They had brought into focus the economic drain and prepared the ground for the Swadeshi Movement. Their nationalism was not based on shallow sentiments, fleeting emotions or abstract ideas of liberty. It was rooted in deep analysis of the complex nature of imperialism and the clash of interest between the Indian people and British rule.

The seeds of nationalism had been sown. In Bengal, a revolutionary group started taking roots and resorted to violence. A group of young nationalists emerged from within Congress, which now had two schools of thought – the moderates, consisting of older Congress leaders, and the extremists, consisting of new thinkers who were louder and more aggressive in their protest and would not settle for anything less than self-government. Among these extremists were Aurobindo Ghose from Bengal and Bal Gangadhar Tilak from Maharashtra, who emerged with a new, unbending spirit.

The British plunder caused a series of famines in India. The picture here shows cooks preparing a meal at a famine relief camp in Madras in 1876.

A NEW FORCE

1876 Famine in Various Parts of India • **1897** Plague in Maharashtra • **1897** Diamond Jubilee of Queen Victoria • **1905** Partition of Bengal Announced

> "Swaraj is my birthright
> and I shall have it."
>
> Bal Gangadhar Tilak, giving a new slogan
> to the national movement

Bal Gangadhar Tilak represented the new sturdy spirit of nationalism. The promise shown by this liberal thinker through his uncompromising determination put the spotlight on Maharashtra, his area of political activity. People admired his deep sensitivity towards the masses, and his groundbreaking approach to win freedom. While Tilak was in jail, eloquent tributes were paid to him at the Amraoti Congress Session in 1897. The best among these was from Surendranath Banerjee, to which the entire Congress gave a standing ovation. Tilak's name echoed and re-echoed, accompanied by such loud cheers that even the voice of the speaker was drowned. The meeting was highlighted in the newspapers the next day. Tilak was a tall leader with a fiery unbending approach towards nationalism. With him, the extremists emerged dramatically on the political scene.

Tilak was born on 23rd July 1856, in a Maharashtrian family in the coastal town of Ratnagiri. His early education began at home under the strict supervision of his father Gangadhar Pant. From the very beginning, Tilak showed an independent spirit, preferring to do everything by himself. From a very early age, he demonstrated a keen interest in Sanskrit and a special aptitude for mathematics.

During his childhood, an incident brought forth his clarity of thought. When a group of young boys was confronted by the gardener for stealing mangoes in a government-owned orchard, Tilak justified the action by arguing that if the orchards belonged to the government, the fruit rightfully belonged to its ryot or the public, therefore it was not a crime to pick mangoes from a sarkari orchard. He could not tolerate injustice in any form or measure.

Tilak knew how to take criticism from an early age. When some classmates made fun of his puny physique, he decided to work on his fitness and joined the *akhara* to become a strong muscular man. With the same resolve, he mastered Sanskrit, mathematics, history and astrology. In college, he studied law and began to do legal practice with his friend Vishnu Shastri Agarkar.

EDUCATION AND THE PRESS

Both Agarkar and Tilak thought alike. They believed it was essential to overcome illiteracy to gain freedom, as education was crucial to awaken political consciousness. Under the National Education Scheme, Tilak established the New English School in 1880, aiming to promote the ideas of patriotism. He also furthered the ideals of the Deccan Education Society, with emphasis on the glory and greatness of Indian culture. Future developments, he believed, must be based on the strong foundation of one's own traditions. He told people that Swaraj was only possible if people relied on their own strength. Tilak proclaimed Swaraj or complete independence as the only goal worth fighting for.

To propagate his ideas, Tilak founded two newspapers: *Kesari* in Marathi and *Maratha* in English. His friend M.B. Namjoshi managed to find a printing machine, but when they wanted to install it at a friend's house, the landlord refused to give permission. In the middle of the night, he quietly carried the machine to a nearby school building. Tilak and

Namjoshi worked through the night to assemble it. In the morning, Namjoshi, Tilak and Agarkar went from door to door to distribute the first issue of *Kesari*, which was different from all other newspapers. It described the actual state of India and its people. Tilak's articles encouraged patriotic sentiments, and provided a fearless criticism of British policies, earning him the title "Bharat Kesari". He typified selfless patriotism, indomitable courage and fierce determination.

CULTURAL SYMBOLS AND NATIONAL PRIDE

Tilak had long realized that the power of a nation lay in its masses, therefore he planted the seed of nationalism in the hearts of the masses. For this, he chose to revive the popular festivals that already lived in the hearts of people. Ganpati festival, an old religious institution in Maharashtra, was celebrated with greater fervour than ever before. He transformed it into a national event. The aim was to utilize the religious sentiments and the historical traditions to regenerate patriotism and a nationalist spirit. Tilak knew it would also provide a forum for the educated classes to come together with the masses, where the former could gain deeper insight into the problems of the illiterate. The festival was given a patriotic touch. The songs sung were on patriotic themes, which aroused deep sentiments of love for the country. As expected, people of all castes and religions joined the processions with great fervour. Sports and merry making were preceded by debates and elocution contests. Celebrated from 1893, the festival gained popularity across the state over the next few years.

Tilak found ways of using cultural symbols and historical heroes to evoke nationalism. He chose Shivaji and underlined the importance of celebrating his birth anniversary, on 15th March, as a national event. During the celebrations, learned discourses were held, eulogizing the heroism of Shivaji and highlighting his relevance in the present political context.

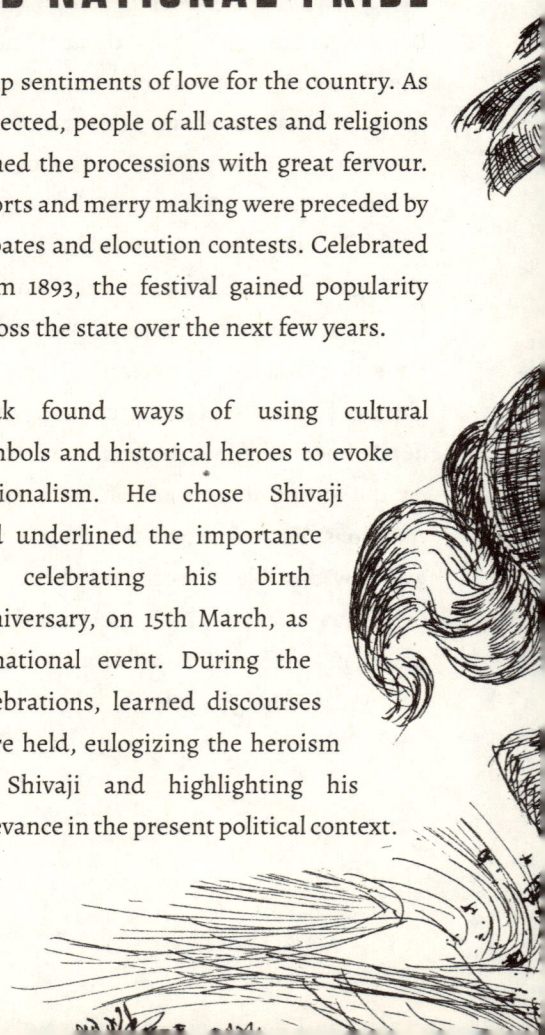

Shivaji Maharaj

Meanwhile, a terrible famine struck the nation in 1896. Hungry men looted grain shops and cried for help. Tilak came to their rescue and encouraged the suffering public to demand benefits offered by the Famine Relief Code as their right. He pressed them not to pay dues to the government by selling their land and cattle. He went from shop to shop, urging shopowners to reduce the price of grain so that the poor could buy it. Week after week, he wrote articles in *Kesari*, urging people to overcome their timidity and become self-reliant. "Why loot the bazaars," he said, "go to the collector and ask him to give you work and food, which is his duty." Instead of helping the suffering lot, the government began to arrest volunteers who were helping the famine victims. Tilak became *"Lokmanya"* meaning the respected one and was blacklisted as the government's "enemy number one".

In 1897, as the plague spread like wildfire in Maharashtra, Tilak and his followers directed their efforts to set up a relief camp to tend to the sick. They treated and nursed the sick, and provided food to the hungry. Around the same time, the British government posted the Indian Civil Services officer, Walter Charles Rand, to Poona as the Plague Commissioner. Shockingly, Rand ordered his officers to remove all plague victims from the town. His officers raided homes indiscriminately and handled the sick roughly. They separated children from mothers, insulted women, defiled the sacred rooms in homes and destroyed property. Even healthy people were picked up and thrown-in with the diseased. Tilak respectfully made appeals to the officers, condemning the ways of Rand. But it had no effect on the government.

MURDERS AND TRIALS

To add to the insult, Rand organized a grand celebration to mark the Diamond Jubilee of Queen Victoria's reign on 22nd June 1897. Grand fireworks were on display, while millions were suffering and dying. The sight of such gaiety for a distant queen at a time like this angered the public. In a fit of rage, three brothers, Damodar Hari Chapekar, Balkrishna Hari Chapekar and Vasudeo Hari Chapekar, shot Charles Rand and another officer Lieutenant Charles Ayerst. The news of the murder shocked the British. The vengeful ruler imposed heavier taxes and stricter laws to punish the citizens. Tilak was the first leader to boldly propose non-payment of taxes. He insisted that the poor peasants should refuse to pay revenue whenever their crops failed due to drought.

The British held Tilak indirectly responsible for Charles Rand's murder. They accused Tilak of inspiring the murder by his stirring speeches and provocative writings, which kindled criminal insurgence. Tilak was convicted on charges of sedition and sentenced to eighteen months of rigorous imprisonment. A phenomenal upsurge of indignation swept through the country. Bazaars remained closed, untutored mill-hands fasted in protest and students wore black-bands to demonstrate against the court's verdict. Slogans such as "Tilak Maharaj Ki Jai" (Salutations to our revered Tilak) bade a touching farewell to this tall leader.

Meanwhile, the Chapekar brothers were sentenced to death. Vasudeo, who escaped arrest, killed two police informants by the name of Dravid brothers, for revealing their plan to kill Rand to the British. He met with the same fate.

When Damodar Hari was being taken to the gallows, he wished to meet Tilak who was imprisoned in the same jail. Chapekar broached his desire to die with the *Bhagavad Gita* in his hand. Tilak handed his own copy of the *Gita* to him. A proud Chapekar met his death with the following lines:

During the jail term, Tilak devoted his time to writing. He came up with a theory on the origin of the Aryans and made an attempt to determine the Vedic period based on the description of stars in the Vedas. His book *The Arctic Home in the Vedas* draws from his knowledge of the Vedas.

Later when he was deported to the notorious Mandalay Jail in the Andaman Islands, commonly known as *Kaala Paani*, for six years, Tilak wrote a commentary on the Gita – *Srimad Bhagwat Geeta Rahasya* in two volumes. With water all around the jail premises, there was no escape for prisoners. Inmates were put in cells as small as 4.5 x 2.7 meters and made to suffer rigorous physical work such as crushing 30 pounds of coconut and mustard a day.

Tilak's trial and conviction set a new trend in nationalism. Sacrifice and suffering for the cause of freedom was the new line of action. Oratory and discussions were replaced by defying measures to challenge British imperialism.

"If you die in this battle of freedom, the glory of heaven will be yours; and if you succeed in this battle, freedom will be yours."

LEADER OF THE MASSES

So far only a platform for intellectual debates, Congress remained distant from the masses. Tilak's writings, speeches and close contact with the masses changed the outlook of political activists. As a result of the involvement of ordinary people, Congress was transformed into an active force. People developed a new self-assertiveness. Tilak's efforts were supported by Aurobindo Ghose, and B.C. Pal in Bengal and Lala Lajpat Rai in Punjab. They advocated that nationalism should be treated as a religion. The new radical thinkers believed in taking up arms against the British, which was a great departure from the politics of the moderates.

Tilak could never accept that India was not ready for self-government. "Swaraj is my birthright" summed up his nationalist thinking. To the nationalists, constitutional agitation held no meaning. The extremists believed that a foreign ruler could not have benevolent intentions towards its subjects. Tilak himself had never expressed any faith in the British sense of justice. All along,

Gokhale had tried to keep the movement steady by remaining a law-abiding activist. However, it was Tilak who made Swaraj the only goal of India.

The involvement of the masses and the increasing political activity was a cause of worry for the British. Unable to tolerate pickets and petitioners, Viceroy Lord Curzon struck a hard blow. He decided to divide Bengal under the façade of smoother administration. Here again, their divide and rule policy was at play. The British wanted to create a Muslim block to widen differences between the two communities. The entire scheme was hatched in secrecy. None of the Congress leaders were involved.

On 16th October 1905, Lord Curzon announced the Partition of Bengal. The entire nation – leaders and masses, Hindus and Muslims – rose against this partition with the loud battle cry of "Vande Mataram!".

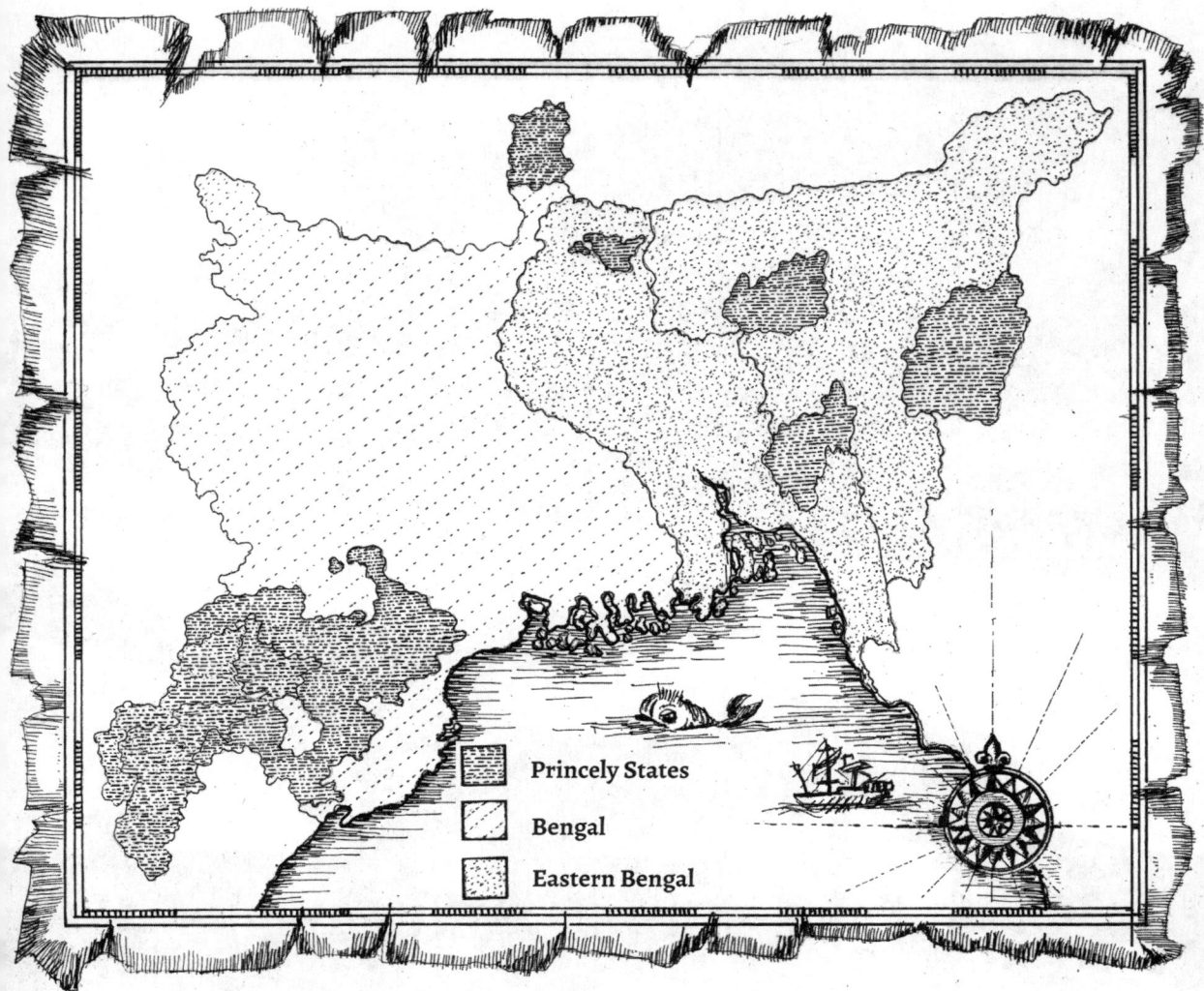

Not to scale. The illustrated map is for approximate reference
purposes only.

	Princely States
	Bengal
	Eastern Bengal

THE RISING TIDE

1905 Swadeshi Movement • **1909** Morley Minto Reforms
• **1914** First World War • **1916** Lucknow Congress

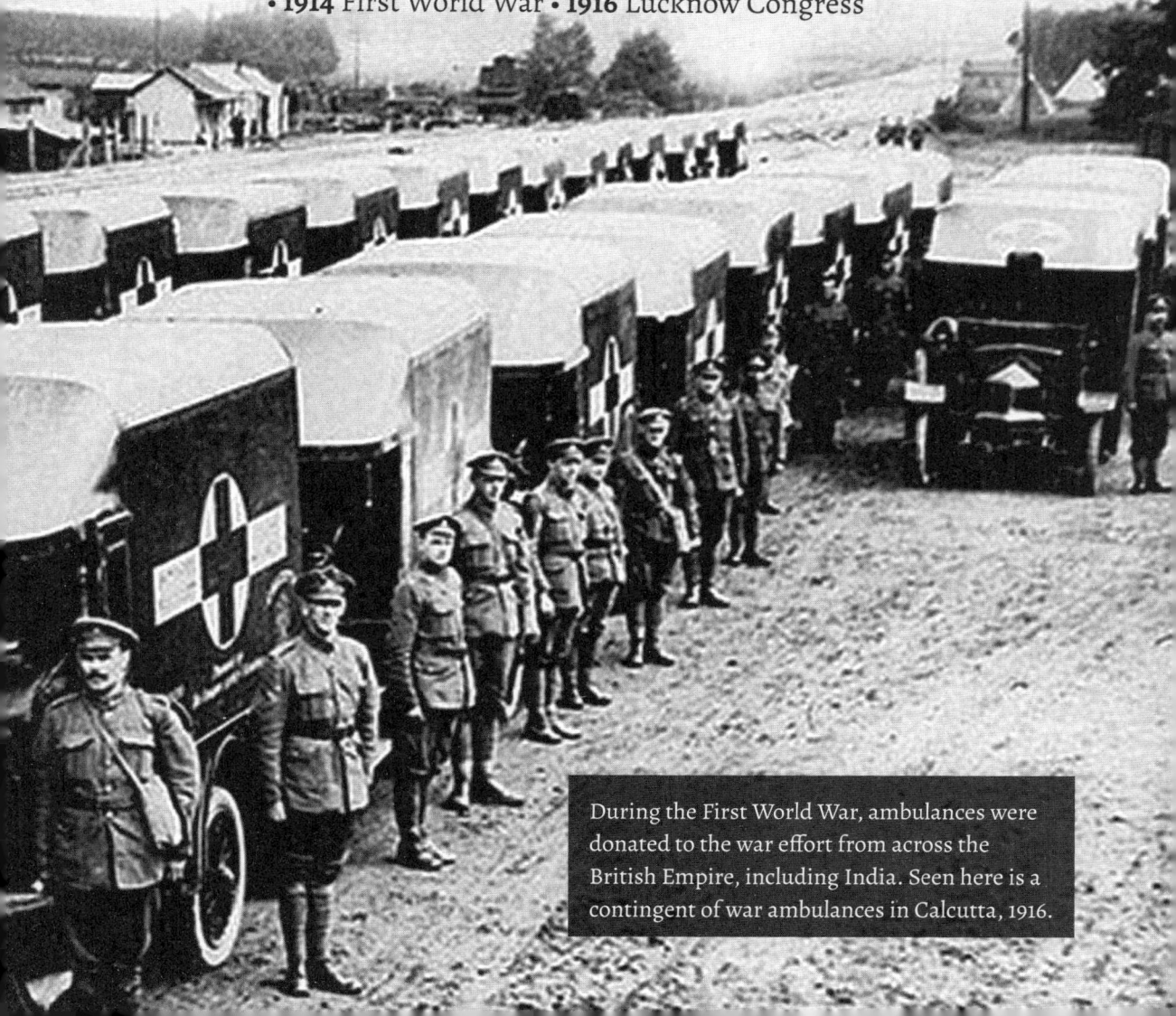

During the First World War, ambulances were donated to the war effort from across the British Empire, including India. Seen here is a contingent of war ambulances in Calcutta, 1916.

"Vande Mataram!" roared the crowd as it marched towards the town hall. The same cry resounded from a nearby street as another group joined in. Black flags inscribed with "No Partition" and "Unity is Strength" fluttered in the calm October breeze as people gathered for a mass meeting. The town hall area in Calcutta saw a sea of more than 50,000 people, with black flags sticking out like boat masts, and waves of "Vande Mataram" surging through the air. Shops were shut, businesses suspended and schools and colleges remained closed. There was a hartal in the town.

Sixteenth October 1905 was a day of mourning in Bengal. Hindus and Muslims tied rakhis on each other's wrists, and proceeded, side by side, to the town hall. Bengal stood united. The rich and the poor, Hindus and Muslims, pleaders and *babus* stood shoulder to shoulder. In one voice, they demanded the annulment of the Partition of Bengal.

Thus, began the Vande Mataram Movement. It was an undeclared war against the government – a psychical force pitted against physical force. Vande Mataram became the war cry, the symbol of patriotism, a stimulus to rise against British imperialism. The movement also saw the boycott of English goods and picketing of foreign shops, in line with the idea of swadeshi.

The boycott started from Bengal and spread all over India. Cloth produced in Manchester, England, became its chief target. Khadi, the Indian-made coarse handspun cloth, was seen as the true symbol of the Swadeshi Movement. Young students picketed foreign goods shops selling commodities like salt, sugar, shoes and cloth, requesting people not

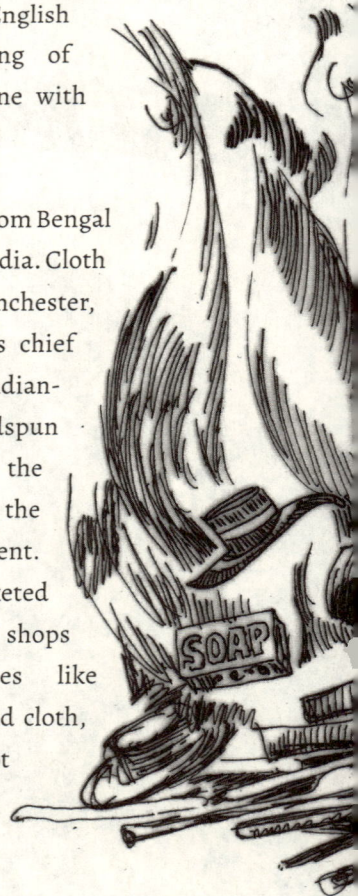

shoes and cloth, requesting people not to buy non-Indian products. In some cases, when the shopkeepers refused to return foreign goods, the volunteers paid for the items and destroyed these goods in community bonfires.

SPIRIT OF PATRIOTISM

During Kali Puja, the Brahmins chanted mantras preaching communal harmony and promoted the use of swadeshi. Priests refused to perform *puja* with foreign material, washer men refused to wash foreign cloth. A little girl of six even refused to swallow foreign medicine despite a serious illness. Commodities such as clothes, shoes, hats and processed food items became regular offerings in the sacred fire for Swaraj or self-rule, performed with the chanting of Vande Mataram.

The spread of the Vande Mataram Movement unnerved the government. Students bore the brunt of the government's repressive measures. Schools and colleges that encouraged nationalism lost government grants, students were expelled, severely beaten and fined. A boy of ten was dragged to the whipping triangle in a marketplace when he was found singing Vande Mataram. A house was pulled down because Vande Mataram was scribbled on one of its posts. The cry of Vande Mataram was forbidden, newspapers like *Bande Mataram* and *Yugantar* were fined for publishing seditious articles, and mass meetings were banned.

Poets and writers feverishly created patriotic literature. In the south, Subramania Bharati inspired patriotism through his lyrical poems and songs. Bengal was also full of such examples. The words of the slogan – "Vande Mataram" – were penned by Bankim Chandra Chatterjee, in his play *Anandmath*, in which he painted a glorious picture of his motherland.

'The Motherland is our only mother. Our Motherland is higher than heaven. Mother India is our mother. We have no other mother. We have no father, no brother, no sister, no wife, no children, no home, no hearth – all we have is the Mother.'

Bankim Chandra Chatterjee, in his book *Anandmath*

RABINDRANATH TAGORE

Another poet whose inspiring swadeshi songs, matchless in melody, gave expression to people's feelings was Rabindranath Tagore. One of the greatest artists of the twentieth century, Tagore chose to play a role in the freedom struggle through the medium of art. He idolized the country in his poems. Every note he wrote rang with deep love for the country. He preached the message of nationalism to people through songs; his plays and ballets aroused nationalist feelings. Tagore rejected the British system of education and considered it antisocial. In light of such views, a National Council for Education was established on 10th November 1905.

Tagore founded Santiniketan in 1901 with the objective of teaching love for Indian art and culture. Like other national schools, he preached self-reliance (atma-shakti), which was best achieved by swadeshi.

Bengal National College was set up under the new education policy and Aurobindo Ghose became its principal. In Maharashtra, the Deccan Educational Society furthered the National Education programme. Science and technology found a place in the curriculum and regional languages became the favoured medium of instruction.

AUROBINDO GHOSE

Aurobindo Ghose introduced the idea of passive resistance. He preached nationalism with a religious fervour and regarded patriotism as a form of devotion. Ghose took politics to a higher plane of spirituality. He wrote articles in *Vande Mataram* and *New India*, directing the spirit of nationalism towards the goal of Swaraj.

to everything Indian. Tilak established the Vastu Pracharini Sabha in Poona. Similar messages were passed on throughout Punjab. In Bengal, Tagore supported swadeshi stores.

"Nationalism is a religion that has come from God. Nationalism is a creed which you shall live... If you are going to be a nationalist, if you are going to assent to this religion of nationalism, you must do it in the religious spirit."

Aurobindo Ghose at a public meeting in Bombay, 1908

Many societies were formed for pushing the boycott movement forward. Boycott went hand in hand with swadeshi. The idea of swadeshi had by now outgrown its original concept of promoting Indian industry. Swadeshi now meant attachment

THE SWADESHI MOVEMENT

The Vande Mataram Movement was gradually transformed into the Swadeshi Movement. The idea of boycott had sprung from the spontaneous upsurge of outrage over the Bengal partition in 1905. Swadeshi followed the same route. Neither of these ideas could have succeeded without the other. Besides, the National Education Programme constituted the third important feature of the movement. The idea behind boycott was mainly an economic one – to put pressure on British industry. Swadeshi also had a strong economic implication for the development of Indian industry.

"Our country is like a tree," wrote Tilak in *Kesari* "of which the original trunk is Swaraj and the branches are swadeshi and boycott." Swadeshi led to Swaraj. The fierce agitation widened into a passive resistance campaign against all forms of foreign rule. Through organized resistance, the mass movement aimed to obstruct the British administration and check oppression.

The ramifications of the Swadeshi Movement were thus four-fold – industrial, educational, cultural and political. Domestic industries such as the Bengal Chemical Factory, Tata Iron and Steel Company, and the Swadeshi Textile Mill, along with cottage industries and various enterprises, helped in national economic growth, which in turn strengthened and supplemented the Swadeshi Movement.

It was not long before the British government realized that a local movement had turned into a nationwide struggle for freedom. It tried to crush the movement with all its force. The repression was not confined to educational institutions and students. The police was now exercising its might everywhere.

In 1905, just six months after the Partition of Bengal, the yearly *Chaitra Mela* was turned into a patriotic event in Bengal. To use this occasion to infuse patriotic fervour among people, the Bengal Provincial Conference organized an event at Raja's *haveli* in Barisal, a mofussil town of Bengal.

A large crowd gathered to see the procession. The path leading to the mansion was lined with policemen armed with regulation lathis – a stout, six-foot-long bamboo stick. Barrister Abdul Rasul, presiding head of the

Conference, and his British wife chanted Vande Mataram all the way. Surendranath Banerjee, Motilal Ghosh and Bhupendranath Bose accompanied the couple barefoot. They managed to reach their destination safely but as soon as the younger delegates reached the gates of the haveli, the police attacked them with lathis. Their badges, which also carried the Vande Matram slogan, were torn off. Barisal town saw a reign of terror, with Gurkha sepoys deployed by the British to crush the patriots. The sepoys also destroyed property, including many swadeshi shops. The tyranny of the British in Barisal fired a spirit of nationalism. People were ready to suffer and sacrifice.

Hindus and Muslims cooperated with each other and became outspoken patriots; stimulated and emboldened by radical newspapers like *Sandhya*, *Yugantar* and *Punjab Kesari*, they jumped into the fray. Leaders like the trio Lala Lajpat Rai from Punjab, Bal Gangadhar Tilak from Maharashtra and Bipin Chandra Pal from Bengal, popularly known as Lal, Bal and Pal, constantly reached out to the masses so that the spirit of swadeshi could be kept alive. It was the idea of swadeshi that brought the movement from the realm of theory to ground-level politics.

"Government repression meant to stifle a movement and suppress a people actually results often in strengthening and steeling them, and thus preparing them for final victory,"

Jawaharlal Nehru, in his book *Glimpses of World History*

CRACKS IN THE CONGRESS

In the Congress sessions of Calcutta and Banaras in 1906, both moderates and extremists denounced the British policies towards India in one voice. Gokhale called

partition a "cruel wrong" of the British government. Muslims joined their Hindu brothers against the British. Nawab Khwaja Atiqullah, brother of Nawab

Salimullah of Dacca and supporter of the British government, made a public declaration that both communities should unite in their protest. The extremists won over the public with their persuasive nationalism.

However, the extensive use of boycott created open differences between the two sections of Congress. The moderates differed on the use of boycott as a political weapon. Gokhale pointed out that while the idea of swadeshi was welcome, the boycott implied a "vindictive desire to injure the other".

> "While it was perfect to fight immediate injustice in Bengal its expansive use may create unnecessary ill-will."
> Moderates, speaking of the boycott

For the extremists, it was a necessary political weapon, a training in self-sufficiency essential for attaining Swaraj. The tempo of the movement rose with the imprisonment of Lala Lajpat Rai and Ajit Singh in Punjab and prosecution of newspapers such as *Sandhya* and *Vande Mataram*. In an important development, Bipin Chandra Pal, a moderate, moved to the extremist camp and was later jailed for advocating nationalism in public. The wind blew in favour of Tilak. As his chances of winning the presidency of the Congress seemed assured, the moderates recommended senior leader Dadabhai Naoroji as their candidate. At the age of 82, Naoroji became the President at the Surat Congress in 1907. Differences continued to widen between the extremists and the moderates. The omission of the three major issues underlined by the extremists – national education, swadeshi and boycott – in the memorandum of the Congress proved to be the last straw. Both fractions chose to split. Alarmed by the popularity of the extremists, the British government immediately turned towards the moderates, promising them substantial reforms. Immensely pleased with the reward, the moderates passed a resolution inviting the Prince and Princess of Wales to visit India, promising to control the boycott at the time of the royal visit. By now, boycott and swadeshi had already gained enough popularity across the country. It especially appealed to the youth, the poor classes, and women.

MUSLIMS IN POLITICS

The British had implemented their policy of divide and rule through the partition of Bengal, with some success. The Britishers' main motive was to destroy Bengali solidarity. Before announcing the partition, Lord Curzon had successfully won over Salimullah Khan, the Nawab of Dacca, by advancing him loans at lower interests. The result was the nawab's full support to the partition.

A concrete shape to communal politics was given in 1906 when the foundation of the All-India Muslim League was laid under the leadership of Aga Khan, Nawab Salimullah Khan and Nawab Mohsin-ul-Mulk. The main objectives of the League were to promote feelings of loyalty towards the British among the Muslims, to protect and advance their political rights and to prevent the rise of hostility among Muslims towards any community. The League demanded a separate electorate for the Muslims. The concessions made by Viceroy Minto towards the Muslims and the League were another step to destroy national unity.

Even though communal riots did flare up in Comilla and Mymensingh (both now in Bangaldesh), Bihar and Peshawar (now in Pakistan) after the Bengal partition, many educated Muslims considered Hindu-Muslim unity necessary to free India from the yoke of foreign rule. In Bihar, Liyakat Hussain distributed Urdu pamphlets to rouse

Muslim sentiments and organized the East India Railway strike. Women came out of *purdah* to join processions. Maulana Abul Kalam Azad supported the boycott policy on the revolutionary lines of Aurobindo Ghose.

THE NEW REVOLUTIONARIES

The reign of police terror used to suppress the agitation at Barisal gave impetus to the rise of terrorism in Bengal. Through political murders and burglary, some believed, it was possible to force the British to comply with the demands for self-government. The credit for organizing the first secret society with the intention of overthrowing British rule in India goes to Vasudev Balwant Phadke of Maharashtra. Tilak's aggressive lectures had motivated people to call out injustice through all means. Many youths turned to violence.

However, even within these revolutionaries there were two broad divisions: One group believed in armed conflicts with the help of Indian soldiers or militias from other nations; the other took to individual acts of violence such as murder of British officers, looting government ammunition and treasury. Many secret societies were established to involve young blood. Anusilan Samiti was one such revolutionary organization that thrived under the leadership of Barindra Kumar Ghose, who was Aurobindo's brother. These revolutionary groups gave military training such as shooting and making of bombs, to the youth. They also made plans to procure arms and explosives through large-scale robberies. The government treasury and armoury became their main targets. *Yugantar*, a revolutionary periodical, became a direct medium to spread their message.

Meanwhile, revolutionaries Khudiram Bose and Prafulla Chaki set out for Muzaffarpur to assassinate Chief Presidency Magistrate, Douglas Kingsford. They accused Kingsford of brutal treatment against a group of dynamic young Indians. However, on 30th April 1908, when the two revolutionaries threw the bomb at a carriage, they ended up accidentally killing the wife and daughter of Barrister Pringle Kennedy. Chaki managed to shoot himself on the spot, but Bose was captured and hanged to death on 13th July 1908.

Soon after, in a raid at one of the revolutionary hideouts in Calcutta, bombs, dynamite and cartridges were recovered. Along with thirty-seven other suspects, Aurobindo Ghose, was arrested and charged with conspiracy and for taking up arms against the British government. In what came to be known as the Alipore Conspiracy Case, fifteen revolutionaries were found guilty. Ghose was acquitted and decided to retire from politics to set up an ashram in Pondicherry.

The Alipore Conspiracy Case created a sensation all over the country. Narendra Gosain, one of the revolutionaries, turned approver. He was killed in prison by Kanailal Dutt and Satyen Bose,

Pistol hidden in book

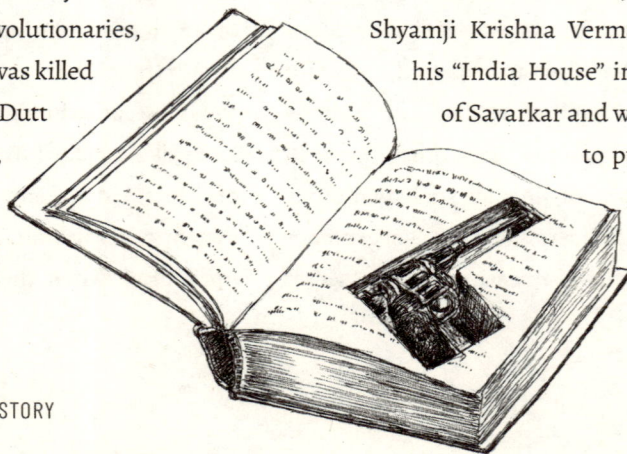

who were also revolutionary prisoners. Promptly, Dutt was hanged. The courage and self-sacrificing spirit of these young men inspired many fellow Indians. These revolutionaries were considered martyrs and songs and poems were dedicated to them as tributes for their extraordinary courage.

Revolutionary activities continued to increase as word spread. Bombay and Poona became the centres of bomb manufacturing. Vinayak Damodar Savarkar laid the foundation of Abhinav Bharat, a secret organization for the youth. He preached the gospel of freedom through *Mitra Mela*, a revolutionary journal. He soon left for London to continue his revolutionary activities and sent arms, cartridges and Mauser pistols from England, hidden in false suitcase bottoms and in between hardbound books. In London, he assisted Shyamji Krishna Verma, who left his "India House" in the hands of Savarkar and went to Paris to publicize the revolutionary literature. Madame Bhikaji Rustam Cama assisted Shyamji and published *Bande Mataram*, an Indian nationalist publication founded by Cama to propagate the injustice of the British government. In spite of being warned, Cama delivered fiery speeches exposing British brutality, at the International Socialist Congress in Paris. During one such speech, Cama was so carried away by emotion that she unfurled the Indian tricolour and hoisted it in the assembly.

Meanwhile, in Nasik, an attempt was made on the life of the Viceroy, and a District Magistrate was shot. In London, a colleague of Savarkar, Madan Lal Dhingra killed Indian Army officer Curzon Wyllie to avenge the hanging of Indians. Before Wyllie was executed, Dhingra said, "The only lesson required in India at present is to learn how to die and the only way to teach it is by dying ourselves. Therefore, I die and glory in my martyrdom."

In Madurai, V.O. Chidambaram Pillai openly spoke for absolute independence under the influence of Bipin Chandra Pal. His arrest led to a serious riot in Tuticorin

and Tirunelveli, where English officer Robert Ashe opened fire on a defiant crowd. As revenge, on 17th June 1911, Ashe was assassinated by R. Vanchi Aiyar of the Bharat Mata Association.

Revolutionary activities continued across the country. Europeans were assaulted in Lahore. In Punjab, Lala Lajpat Rai was prosecuted for his writings in the newspaper *Punjabi*. As a consequence, riots broke out in Rawalpindi. Ajit Singh and Lala Hardayal backed the movement in Punjab with the help of Aga Haider and Syed Haider Riza. Rai's absence put a halt to revolutionary literature for some time but Rash Behari Bose carried on the tradition of revolutionary press through pamphlets, published under the name "Liberty", which were circulated secretly.

Stirring the spirit of swadeshi among the masses, Aurobindo Ghose's *Jugantar pamphlets* preached open revolt and absolute denial of British rule. These pamphlets included instructions for guerrilla warfare. The literature encouraged the growth of revolutionary activity among the youth. Some notable leaders from Delhi, namely

Avadh Behari, Amir Chand and many others, joined the group.

A general plan for armed rebellion was drawn up by Sachindra Nath Sanyal, with the help of Indian soldiers. The revolutionary groups of Bengal were informed and contacts were made with cantonments in north India. Two regiments in Punjab promised to initiate the rebellion. Rash Behari Bose himself went from Benaras to Lahore, but a member of Bose's group betrayed them. Revolutionary hideouts were raided in Lahore, where arms and revolutionary literature was unearthed. Many revolutionaries were captured and tried in what came to be known as the Lahore Conspiracy Case.

Outside India, the revolutionaries involved nations who were hostile to Britain. In Germany, Lala Hardayal began the Indian Independence Committee. The members raised funds to collect arms and smuggle them to Indian revolutionary groups through Afghanistan, with the help of Turkey. In America, the Ghaddar Party carried out anti-imperialistic propaganda and aroused public sympathy.

Individual acts of violence were brutally crushed. Even though they did not always mobilize a mass movement, the revolutionary acts gave rise to fearlessness, spirit of defiance and resistance against British imperialism.

The British crushed the revolutionary uprising and the peaceful Swadeshi Movement by making mass arrests and putting prominent leaders in jail for longer duration. Lala Lajpat Rai was deported. Bal Gangadhar Tilak was charged with seditious writing in *Kesari*. Tilak defended his own case before a partial jury at a historic trial where he spoke for twenty-one hours. He was imprisoned and sent to Mandalay Jail in Burma. With Lal, Bal, Pal jailed and British suppression in full swing, the movement touched a low ebb. Disharmony between the Hindus and the Muslims further weakened the fight for freedom.

MORLEY-MINTO REFORMS

Around this time, Lord Minto succeeded Lord Curzon as the Viceroy. Like his predecessors, he continued to play the game of divide and rule. When Aga Khan, leader of the Muslim League, urged Minto to secure a suitable communal electorate, the Viceroy made full use of the opportunity and devised new reforms together with Lord Morley, Secretary of State for India, in 1909.

The Morley-Minto reforms allowed for more representation of Indians in the Provincial Council. An Indian was appointed as a member of the Governor-General's Executive Council and another one in the Provincial Executive Council. The electorate comprised of non-official members of the Provincial Legislative Council, landlords and eminent individuals from universities and the field of commerce. Under the new law, Muslims, landlords and European capitalists got reserved seats. Women had no right to vote. The governors had the power to exclude any individual as politically undesirable.

The powers of the Legislature were limited. Areas of public interest like the army and the native states were excluded from debate. Discussions were allowed only on matters of finance and budget.

The Congress disapproved of communal electorates. Even the otherwise accommodating moderates felt disappointed as the reforms did not allow for a parliamentary form of government. The extremists openly attacked separatism which was to strike a blow at the nationalist movement.

In 1911, Lord Hardinge attempted to placate Indians by repealing the Partition of Bengal. However, it was too little too late. A series of regressive acts such as the Press Act of 1910 and the Special Tribunals Law Amendment Act of 1908 were put in place to impose restrictions on newspapers, curbing the freedom of press, expression and growth of nationalism.

Lord Minto and
Lord John Morley

FIRST WORLD WAR

In 1914, Great Britain declared war against Germany. Even though India had no grievance against Germany, it had no choice but to participate in the war.

"She (India) was forced to toe the line of her imperialist mistress."
Jawaharlal Nehru, in *The Discovery of India*, 1946

As the Allies (mainly comprising of France, Great Britain, Russia, Italy and Japan) declared war on the Ottoman Empire, Great Britain fought Turkey (which was part of the Central Powers). This displeased the Muslims, who regarded the Caliph of Turkey as their Sultan.

More and more soldiers were recruited from India. The princes and upper middle class declared loyalty to the British in the hope that help rendered to the British government in their hour of need might achieve suitable rewards in the future. But the strain was felt by the poor the most as India's resources were being used up. They were jobless and subjected to the oppressing demands of joining the army. To escape forced recruitment, many Indians left the

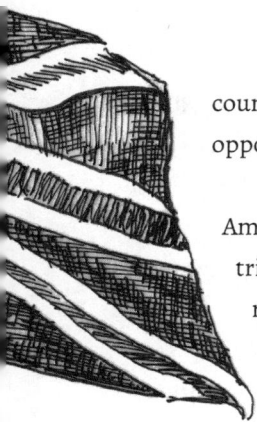

country in search of jobs and better opportunities.

Among the many who desperately tried to escape this forced recruitment was a group of Punjabis who sailed in a ship called *Komagata Maru* to Canada. The steamship was not allowed to dock and turned away from the port itself by the Canadian government, which was an English ally. Despite being British subjects Indians onboard this ship were refused basic amenities such as rations for their return journey by the Canadian government. After

waiting for two months at the port, the group was allowed to return home, with several killed and shot on their way back home. The tragic incident bolstered the raging discontent in Punjab.

For India, the singular advantage of the war was that it facilitated industrialization and encouraged foreign investment. The growing strength of Indian capitalism soon became an important factor in the political movement. The pre-war and early war lull in politics was a thing of the past as the demand for self-government gained ground once again.

HOME RULE

Bal Gangadhar Tilak resumed the demand for Swaraj after completing his long prison term. With leading moderates such as Gopal Krishna Gokhale and Pherozeshah Mehta already dead, the Bombay Congress heartily welcomed the extremists and set the stage for a new nationalist movement.

A new entrant to the political scene was Annie Besant, who first visited India in 1893 and decided to settle in the country. She had great reverence for Indian culture and devoted herself to the Indian cause. She founded the Home Rule League in 1916 and became its first president. A new figure in politics, Besant was well known for her work at the Theosophical Society.

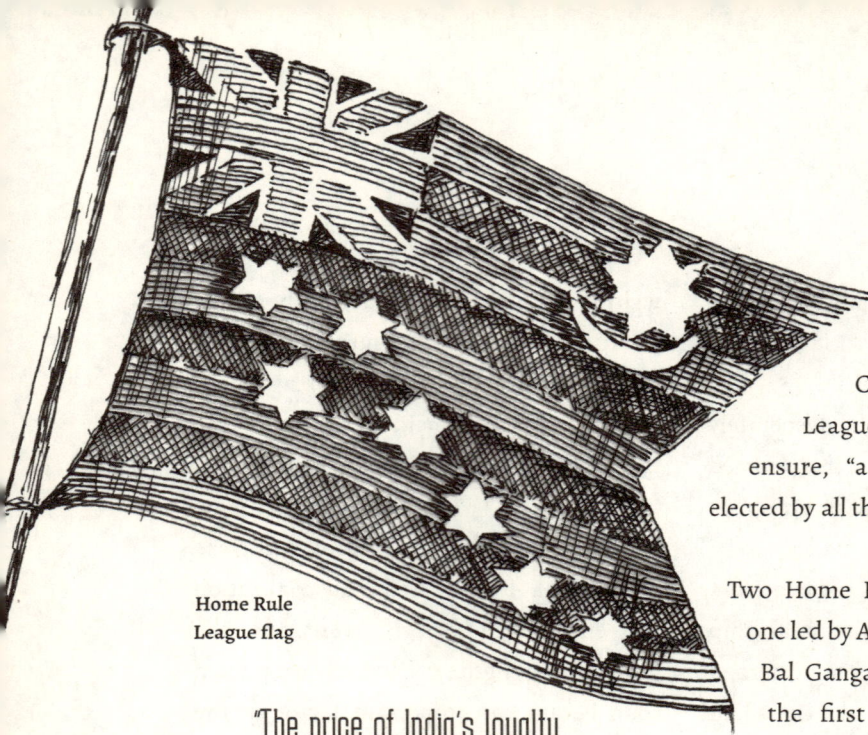
Home Rule
League flag

govern. An auxiliary of the Indian National Congress, the Home Rule League of India, she hoped, would ensure, "a government by councils, elected by all the people."

Two Home Rule Leagues were formed, one led by Annie Besant and the other by Bal Gangadhar Tilak. Besant became the first woman President of the Congress as many Home Rule Leagues began functioning from Bombay, Kanpur, Allahabad, Calicut, Ahmedabad, Madras, etc. They infused a fighting spirit and attracted the young. In the years to follow, the Congress saw yet another woman president, Sarojini Naidu.

"The price of India's loyalty is India's freedom,"

Annie Besant during one of her public speeches

She also published a newspaper called *New India*, from Madras, expressing her confidence in the Indian capability to self-

HINDU-MUSLIM UNITY

The Lucknow Congress, in 1916, marked the revival of the Indian National Congress. Annie Besant, Lokmanya Tilak and other extremists were welcomed into the party. The session was marked by a revival of the Hindu-Muslim unity. Tilak played an important role in bringing the two communities together by maintaining that unity was essential to attain freedom from the British. In his eagerness to achieve unity, he accepted the policy of separate electorates and weightage secured by the Muslim community. The number of Muslim members in the legislature was laid down province by province.

The Muslim League also became more accommodative of Hindu views largely because of their exasperation at the British oppression. The party was upset with the ruler over the shutting down of two Urdu newspapers, Maulana Abul Kalam Azad's *Al-Hilal* and Maulana Mohammed Ali Jauhar's *Comrade* under the Press Act of 1914. The Congress and the League jointly demanded abolition of the Indian Council, election of four-fifths of central and provincial Legislative Council members, a promise of non-interference in provincial matters and full control over the Central government.

One delegate at the meeting received much attention. Humbly draped in khadi, he had recently returned from South Africa after achieving success in his attempts to fight British imperialism. Mohandas Karamchand Gandhi spoke not about politics but about the social evils ailing Indian society, and the virtue of cleanliness and labour. People were mesmerized to hear him speak about charkha as an instrument of economic independence. In contrast, his speech dampened the high expectations of many Congress stalwarts. Little did they realize that a new star shone on the horizon of India's freedom struggle. Gandhi was to spearhead a unique movement in the years to come.

"Everywhere there was a lively expectation of change. The political barometer was rising..."
Jawaharlal Nehru, in his book *Nehru: The First Sixty Years Vol I*

THE MAN WHO CHANGED IT ALL

1915 Gandhi Returns to India • **1917** Champaran Satyagraha • **1918** Montagu-Chelmsford Reforms • **1922** Chauri Chaura Incident • **1928** Bardoli Satyagraha

Gandhi's entry into the freedom struggle was a turning point in history. Seen here is the young lawyer in South Africa who introduced the world to satyagraha.

"A leader of his people, unsupported by any outward authority: a politician whose success rests not upon craft nor the mastery of technical devices, but simply on the convincing power of his personality; a victorious fighter who has always scorned the use of force, a man of wisdom and humility, armed with resolve and inflexible consistency, who has devoted all his strength to the uplifting of his people and the betterment of their lot, a man who has confronted the brutality of Europe with the dignity of the simple human being, and thus at all times risen superior."

Albert Einstein on Mahatma Gandhi, 1939

Known for living like a saint, Gandhi was given the name "Mahatma" by Rabindranath Tagore, and "Bapu" for his abundant love for people.

In the small town of Porbandar in Gujarat, Karamchand Gandhi and Putlibai were blessed with a son on 2nd October 1869. In his early years, Mohandas imbibed the principles of truth from his father and grandfather, and reverence for Hindu traditions from his religious mother. He learnt early in life that the practice of speaking truth gave one immense inner strength.

As a child, Mohandas did not hesitate to write an apology to his father when he stole some gold from his mother's bangle. Mohandas's faith in truth was cemented when his father praised him for speaking the truth, with tears of appreciation.

According to existing customs of the time, Mohandas was married to Kasturbai when he was in high school. Nurturing a strong desire to study further, he sailed off to England. Before leaving, he vowed to his mother that he would keep away from alcohol, meat and women. To remain a vegetarian was not easy in a cold, distant land. Despite facing difficulties in finding vegetarian food, he stuck to his word.

While in London, Mohandas grew interested

in Hindu philosophy and studied the *Bhagavad Gita*. The English sense of cleanliness impressed him and he began to see the unhygienic practices being carried out back home. From here, he came up with his principles of self-help. As promised, he returned home after three years as a barrister, but soon set off for South Africa to look for work.

In those days, thousands of Indians had emigrated to South Africa as merchants and labourers. They were discriminated against and treated with disrespect and hostility. Most of them were called indentured (termed after the legal document they carried) labourers who had come to South Africa voluntarily. Many of them were considered "untouchables" back home, and had been dealing with starvation in their own country. However, their arrival in South Africa was like being out of the frying pan and into the fire! Here too, these peasants suffered humiliation and poverty. They had to carry an identity pass with them at all times. Anyone found without these passes could be arrested at any time. Indians were

not allowed to buy or own land or travel in first-class coaches. Regularly kicked out from footpaths, these indentured workers had to pay three pounds per person to reside in what looked like slums. They were legally barred from buying South African gold.

Gandhi arrived in South Africa in 1893. By 1896, the National Legislature of South Africa denied voting rights to Asians. For Gandhi, this was distressing. He got in touch with a group of Indians and urged them to fight against these rules. At the age of twenty-four, he gave his first public speech.

Replica of an Emigration pass

DEPOT No. 3123

FORM NO. 44.
Ship No. 980

625 97

MAN'S
EMIGRATION PASS.

HEALTH CLASS.

For Steam Ship GANGES.

proceeding to South Africa.

MADRAS, 15 April 1912.

Name	H. Murli
Father's name	R. Hari
Age	30 years
Caste	Nair
Height	5 feet 8 inches
Name of nect-of-kin	M. Prabhu (son)
If married. to whom	S. Rajlaxmi
District	Kottayam
Taluq	Kottayam
Village	Veloor
Bodily marks	A scar on left hand / Mole on left cheek
Occupation in India	Farmer
Chest Measurement	30 1/2"

Certified that we have examined and passed the above-named man as fit to emigrate; that he is free from all bodily and mental disease; and that he has been vaccinated since engaging to emigrate.

Surgeon Superintendent.

Depot Surgeon.

Certified that the man above described has appeared before me and has been engaged by me on behalf of the Government of South Africa as willing to proceed to that country to work for hire, and that I have explained to him all matters concerning his engagement and duties.

Government Emigration Agent for South Africa.

Permitted to proceed as in a fit state of health to undertake the voyage to South Africa.

Madras--15-4-12

Protector of Emigrants.

For the next few years, Gandhi laboured quietly, giving up his profession and personal belongings. He set up Tolstoy Farm, the first Indian ashram in South Africa, and was also responsible for establishing the first Indian settlement in the country, called the Phoenix Settlement.

From here, he preached his doctrine of love, truth, self-help and discipline. He reinforced these principles through his articles in the *Indian Opinion* and inspired people to resist all insult to their self-esteem and oppression in any form. In 1906, a straight blow fell upon Indians in the form of the Asiatic Registration Act,

Tolstoy Farm

which forced Asians, including Indians, to register themselves with the authorities like criminals. This deeply angered the Asians. Gandhi became their leader and channelized their anger into a firm demand to repeal the law. The resistance was peaceful and nonviolent in nature. Collectively, the people bore police torture but not one raised a hand to retaliate. They suffered the agony of violence but did not respond with aggression. They, however, remained firm on their demand. Gandhi was jailed along with thousands of Indians. It was not long before the authorities yielded and Gandhi's satyagraha won.

SATYAGRAHA

Armed with the weapon of nonviolence and satyagraha, Gandhi returned to his motherland in January 1915.

Satyagraha or "holding onto truth" in Gandhi's own words is "the vindication of truth, not by infliction of suffering on the opponent, but on one's own self." Satyagraha is the truth force that requires self-control. This principle became the guiding light of his resistance against aggression. He believed that the acts of violence only create bitterness in the survivors and brutality in the destroyers. His philosophy of satyagraha aimed to exalt both sides.

Gandhi listed out the attributes of a satyagrahi in his weekly newspaper *Young India*, where he mentioned that a satyagrahi bids goodbye to fear. He stated that it is a weapon of the brave, not of cowards.

Thus, satyagraha was an active force that could take various forms like fasting, non-cooperation, civil disobedience and willingness to suffer legal penalties. Therefore, Gandhi did not like the use of the term "passive resistance".

YOUNG INDIA.

PUBLISHED EVERY WEDNESDAY AND SATURDAY.

BOMBAY, SATURDAY, MAY 10, 1919.

RULES FOR A SATYAGRAHI:

1. A Satyagrahi, that is a civil resister, will harbour no anger.
2. He/she will suffer the anger of the opponent.
3. He/she will put up with assaults from the opponent. There is no room for retaliations. Nonviolence is the very foundation of Satyagraha.
4. He/she will submit to arrest when the authorities seek for him.
5. In word, action or thought, he will not insult the authority.
6. In the course of struggle, a government official has to be protected by a Satyagrahi.
7. Satyagrahis will not salute the Union Jack, nor will they insult it.

Gandhi did not engage actively in politics immediately after his return to India. He settled down at the Sabarmati Ashram on the banks of river Sabarmati in Ahmedabad. Clad in his loin cloth, he toured the whole country with his wife to understand the social conditions. Gandhi lived a simple life and became one with the people. Poverty and illiteracy shocked him, social evils like child marriage and untouchability pained him. In his speeches, Gandhi spoke of equality and preached that nobody should be treated as untouchable. Swadeshi was his watchword and charkha became his symbol for freedom. Gandhi believed that cottage industries would not only give employment to the poor but also undermine Britain's economic power.

THE FIRST VICTORY

The poor peasants urged Gandhi to visit Champaran, hoping for some miracle from the peaceful fighter. On 15th April 1917, enroute to Champaran, Gandhi reached Muzaffarpur, where he was received by J.B. Kripalani. The sharecroppers in this region were bound by a law to grow and sell indigo to the British at low prices. Unable to pay land revenues, the Indigo growers suffered penalties. Gandhi found the fear-stricken peasants utterly crushed by the injustice. The courts did not provide any relief either. Along with J.B. Kripalani, Rajendra Prasad, Brij Kishore Babu and Maulana Mazrahul Haq, Gandhi conducted an inquiry into the grievances of the farmers. He demanded a proper hearing and early settlement of cases for the indigo sharecroppers.

His next stop was Motihari in Bihar, where massive crowds gathered to see the emerging leader. When the British government banned his entry, Gandhi defied the orders. He was tried in court and justified his action as obeisance to the Almighty, for the sake of the misery of thousands. Gandhi's imprisonment drew the attention of the entire country. Thousands mobbed government offices to court arrest, letters poured in expressing readiness to join the struggle.

The British government was forced to withdraw the case against Gandhi and also appoint him as a member of the committee looking into the grievances of indigo cultivators. The Champaran settlement was the first victory of satyagraha in India as it resulted in full repayment of money, and twenty-five percent refund to the farmers. The poor, who represented the majority, saw a ray of hope in Gandhi.

> "A little man who looked straight into his (peasant's) eyes, and deep down into his shrunken heart, and sensed his long agony,"
>
> Jawaharlal Nehru, *Glimpses of World History*, 1934

Kasturbai

Thanks to Gandhi's arrival on the political stage, the poor were ready to march out of suffering by fighting for their freedom. Gandhi or Bapu, as he was lovingly called, became a father figure for the masses.

Gandhi and his wife Kasturba, who was now lovingly called Ba (mother), busied themselves in educating the Champaran peasants. They set up medical assistance in the area, and worked towards improving the social conditions of the poor.

Kasturba went from hamlet to hamlet to spread awareness on cleanliness, underlining the need for hygiene in day-to-

day life. Many poor women owned a single sari, which was worn by them at all times, leading to unhygienic conditions. Kasturba taught the underprivileged how to use the charkha. Throughout this journey, Kasturba remained an active follower and supporter of Gandhi on social and political issues.

While Gandhi was still involved in Champaran, he was urgently invited to lead the strike of mill workers in Ahmedabad, who were fighting for increased wages. The workers were afraid and wavered in their resolve. This was the first time Gandhi went on a fast to put forth his demand. The peasants agreed to strike peacefully till an agreement was reached with the British authorities. The peaceful but assertive manner had the desired effect and a settlement was soon arrived at.

Immediately after this, Gandhi began a satyagraha campaign in Kaira district. Under the Land Revenue Rules, the cultivators were entitled to suspension of land revenue if the crops fell below twenty-five percent. However, the British officials denied any such concession to Kaira farmers. With Gandhi by their side, the cultivators, took a pledge not to pay revenues and suffer any consequences, including forfeiture of land. A significant figure of the future, Vallabhbhai Patel, joined Gandhi in this struggle.

Once again, the satyagraha did wonders. The British government was ultimately forced to offer terms acceptable to the cultivators. The peasants won over their fear of legal threats. It marked the beginning of political consciousness among the peasants. By now, people had realized that their salvation lay in satyagraha and that Gandhi was their champion.

MONTAGU-CHELMSFORD REFORMS

After the Lucknow Congress, the Home Rule Movement spread all over India. It placed before the country a concrete proposal for self-government. More and more participation by women heightened the popularity of the movement. Led by Gandhi, the masses actively participated in the struggle.

On 15th June 1917, Annie Besant and two of her colleagues were taken prisoner. The British government was determined to suppress the movement with firmness. The internment of Besant adversely affected the British government's image, which suffered a blow in other countries as well. Both the Congress and the Muslim League considered the proposal of adopting Passive Resistance. Prominent Muslim leaders like Jinnah also joined in.

Gandhi, now a leader, encouraged Hindu-Muslim unity. Sir Subramania Iyer was now at the forefront of the Home Rule League.

GANDHI TAKES CENTRESTAGE

Meanwhile, the British government's policy of playing Hindu-Muslim politics and rallying moderates against extremists was failing. Politically, India was united as never before. There was open defiance against the British government. Some underground revolutionary organizations in Bengal conspired with supporters in Germany and Turkey. The disgruntled Ghadar party in United States, together with the Irish republican movement, expanded their activities to exploit the situation, sparking off unrest. A pan-India mutiny took place in the British Indian Army from Punjab to Singapore, with an aim to overthrow British rule in the Indian subcontinent. Constant pressure by the Congress and the Muslim League resulted in the Montagu-Chelmsford Reforms in 1918 (also called the Montford Report).

The Montford Report provided for a responsible executive at three levels – local bodies, provinces and the Government of India. It suggested complete popular control in the local bodies and relaxation of control in the provinces. However, the Government of India remained wholly responsible to the British Parliament. Law and order was the domain of the government and governors had special powers to overrule the ministers.

(Starting from left) M.K Gandhi, Madan Mohan Malviya, Mohammad Ali Jinnah, Jawaharlal Nehru and Annie Besant

ROWLATT ACT

Lord Chelmsford also appointed a committee to investigate into the extent and nature of criminal conspiracies in the country and asked the committee to suggest suitable measures that could be adopted. Justice Rowlatt was made President of this panel. Like the Sedition Committee formed to look into the acts of sedition, and to penalize newspapers and editors, the Rowlatt Committee held in-camera proceedings. It merely examined facts provided by the Government of India.

Rowlatt Bills were passed on 18th March 1919, imposing drastic regulations which practically denied any legal protection to Indians. Three high court judges forming special courts were eligible to conduct in-camera proceedings to decide on the cases. There could be no further appeal from this court. Numerous protest meetings were held against these "lawless laws" which were thrust upon the people at a time when they were expecting constitutional reforms as a reward of their cooperation in Britain's war efforts.

"Na Appeal, Na Vakil, Na Dalil"
(No appeal, no lawyer, no hearing),
as the leaders described it

A wave of indignation swept across the country.

SILENCE BEFORE THE STORM

Gandhi was determined to resist this "organized tyranny to the uttermost", as he called it. He organized a satyagraha campaign, refusing to obey the oppressive laws under the Rowlatt Act. An appeal for a nationwide strike was made in consultation with Chakravarti Rajagopalachari, another tall leader. Sixth of April was declared as Satyagraha Day – a day of fasting and prayer when all commercial activities were suspended. This was the beginning of the Civil Disobedience Movement. The hartal was a unique success but there were reports of clashes in many places. Gandhi kept reminding people that satyagraha did not have space for any kind of violence, be it pillage or incendiarism.

> "Nobody should plunder shops, extort money, cut telegraph wires or destroy property in the name of satyagraha,"
> Gandhi told the masses

But incidents of violence were reported from all over. Gandhi was hurt and disappointed. He felt people were not yet ready for satyagraha. Declaring that the Civil Disobedience campaign was a "Himalayan miscalculation", Gandhi observed a three-day fast.

Meanwhile, there was trouble brewing in Amritsar. Punjab had been cut off from the rest of the country due to rigid censorship

A deserted marketplace during hartal

of news and strict checking at borders. When Gandhi tried to reach Amritsar, he was stopped at Delhi border and taken by the police to Bombay. It gave rise to the rumour that Gandhi was arrested, leading to more violence. While Gandhi pondered on discontinuing the Civil Disobedience Movement, a spine-chilling event in Amritsar shook people all over the world. It brought into the open the ugly face of British tyranny.

The charkha became the physical embodiment and symbol of Gandhi's Swadeshi Movement and Non-cooperation programme.

THE NON-COOPERATION
MOVEMENT

1919 Jallianwala Bagh • **1919** All India Khilafat Conference • **1919** Government of India Act • **1920** Gandhi Home Rule League President • **1921** Prince of Wales Visits India • **1927** Simon Commission

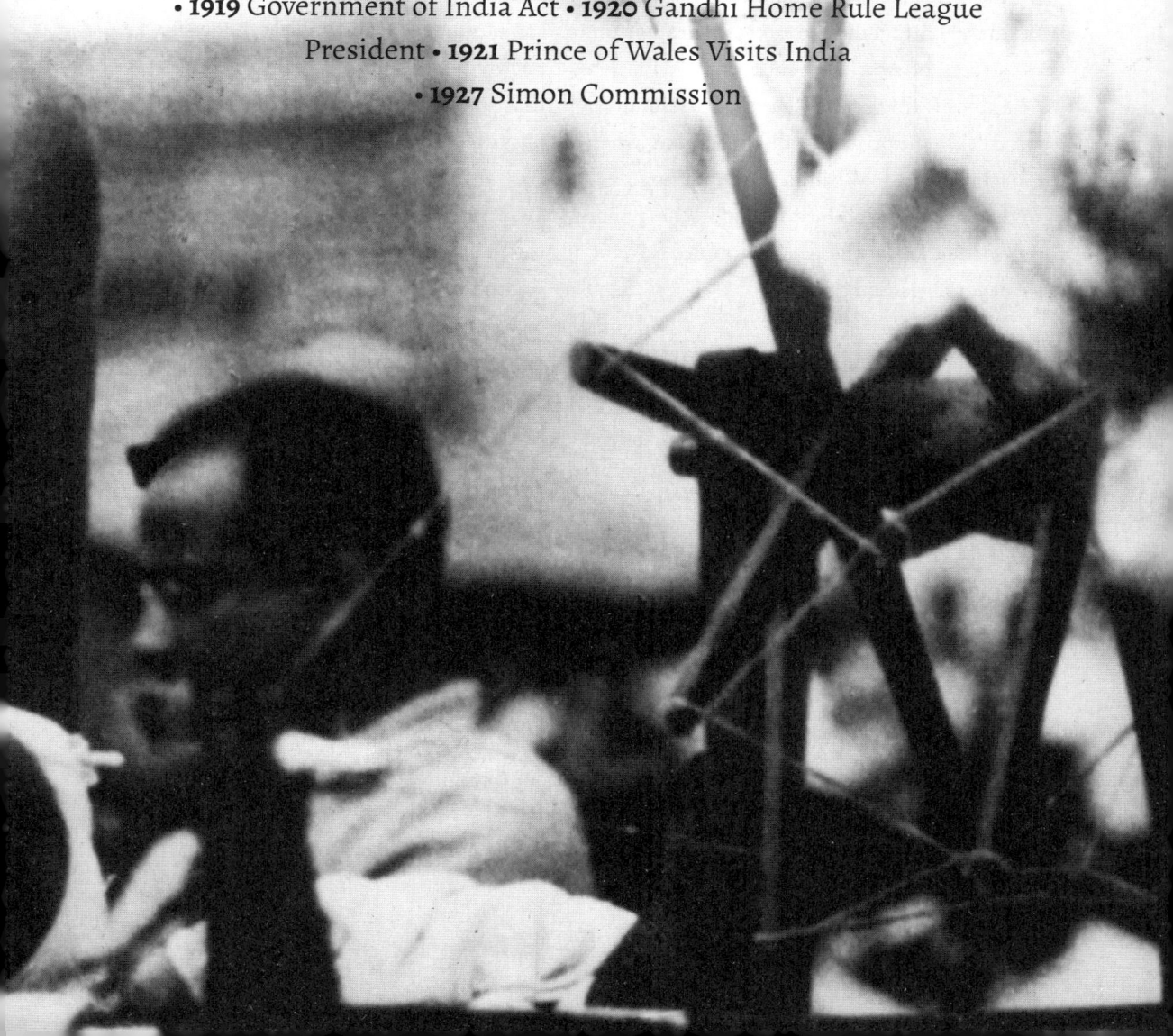

The Satyagraha Day was the beginning of a series of events that shook the nation. On 9th April 1919, when two prominent leaders, Dr. Saifuddin Kitchlew and Dr. Satyapal, were deported from the province, both Hindus and Muslims marched together in protest through the streets of Amritsar, shouting, "Mahatma Gandhi ki Jai" and "Hindu-Musalman ki Jai". On the occasion of Ram Navami, when Hindus and Muslims gathered together in the spirit of brotherhood, the police opened fire at the peaceful crowd, leaving several dead on the spot.

A section of the outraged crowd took its revenge on the Englishmen. The attack left six British men dead, including some bank officials. During the attack, telegraph wires were cut, a railway station was ransacked and a few buildings were destroyed. The angry group also assaulted an English woman named Miss Sherwood. However, she was rescued by some Indians. Following which, peace was restored in the area, making it possible for the funeral procession of the victims to pass off smoothly.

Two days later, Col. Reginald Dyer was called to Amritsar to take control of the volatile situation. Almost immediately, he ordered the arrest of prominent leaders and prohibited processions, meetings and gatherings.

JALLIANWALA BAGH MASSACRE

Meanwhile, a public meeting was organized at Jallianwala Bagh on Baisakhi, 13th April 1919, at 4.30 p.m. General Reginald Dyer was aware of the meeting, but no warning was issued to the gathering nor anyone prevented from going to the meeting. While the meeting was in progress, General Dyer entered the Jallianwala Bagh and stationed his troops at different vantage points. Without any warning, he ordered his troops to fire. Escape routes were few, the soldiers fired from a range of 100 yards on a dense crowd. Incessant firing took place until the ammunition lasted. General Dyer marched off, leaving the dead and the wounded. Two days later, on 15th April 1919, martial law was imposed in Amritsar.

From that day Jallianwala Bagh became a political pilgrimage for all those seeking freedom from foreign rule. Thirteenth April was observed as National Day, while sixth to thirteenth April was declared as National Week.

To add insult to injury, General Dyer issued the infamous "Crawling Order" – any Indian passing through the street where Miss Sherwood had been attacked would have to crawl through the stretch, if the officer on duty so demanded. A whipping post for public flogging was set up to punish those who disobeyed the order. General Dyer's colleague, Captain Doveton, who was incharge of the order, made sure that even schoolboys were not spared from the punishment. As many as 107 people were kept in small enclosures, exposed to the burning sun for defying the order. The regime of martial law brought in a reign of terror, a specimen of British brutality.

The news of ongoing atrocities in Punjab did not immediately reach the country due to closure of state borders. But as soon as it did, people were outraged by the injustice. Gandhi condemned the "crawling order" as absolutely appalling. Despite the distasteful developments, Gandhi decided against resuming the civil disobedience movement,

As many as 120 people (as per official records) jumped into a well to escape British brutality during the Jallianwala incident

as he felt that people were not yet ready to take a peaceful route to fight the injustice.

Pandit Madan Mohan Malviya, an educationist and foremost spokesman of nationalist forces, presented the details of the tragedy with a sense of shock before the Central Legislative Council. As a result of Malviya's queries, the Viceroy ordered an inquiry into the event. Simultaneously, the

Pandit Madan Mohan Malviya

Congress Committee also appointed an inquiry committee which included Motilal Nehru, C.R. Das, Fazl-ul-Haq and Abbas Tyabji.

Coincidentally, the Congress Session was held in Amritsar that year. Under the shadow of the Jallianwala Bagh Tragedy, Gandhi, suggested a countrywide non-cooperation campaign. However, the decision was put on hold by the Congress Committee as the inquiry commission report was still awaited. Despite Gandhi's insistence on non-cooperation, the move was vehemently rejected by Tilak.

THE KHILAFAT MOVEMENT

During this period, the bitterness and anger of Muslims expressed itself strongly in the Khilafat Movement. Early in 1912, the Indian Muslims had started an agitation to pressurize Britain to change her policy towards Turkey.

The Muslims regarded the Sultan of Turkey as their Caliph or religious head. During the war, Turkey supported Germany against Britain. This became particularly awkward for Indian Muslims because their loyalty towards the British came into direct conflict with their religious sentiments. Realizing their unhappiness, the British government

Deposition of the last caliph of Islam Abdulmejid II
by the national Assembly of Ankara, Turkey

assured a sympathetic treatment towards Turkey and its territorial integrity.

However, after the War, the Asiatic portions of the Turkish Empire came under the control of England and France. Even within Turkish dominions, the High Commission of the Allied Powers deprived the Sultan of all authority. This was regarded by Muslims in India as a great betrayal by Britain.

The All India Khilafat Conference was held on 23-24th November 1919, in Delhi. Gandhi was elected its President. He advised the Muslims to protest through boycott and non-cooperation. The decision of the Khilafat Movement was reaffirmed by the Muslim League. At the Khilafat Conference held in Amritsar, it was decided that a deputation represented by both Hindus and Muslims will be sent to the Viceroy. The decision was duly signed by eminent Hindus such as Gandhi, Motilal Nehru, Swami Shraddhanand and Pandit Madan Mohan Malviya. Congress also lent its full support.

Meanwhile, Gandhi issued a manifesto about his future course of action and asserted that the same will be pursued by Khilafatists. The manifesto of the Khilafat Committee was an elaboration of Gandhi's doctrine of nonviolent non-cooperation.

> Even though Gandhi's emphasis on the Khilafat issue was severely criticized by many of his associates, it brought the two communities together.

What set everything off were the two bills introduced by Delhi High Court judge Henry Rowlatt while renewing the Defence of India Act. The first bill allowed judges to convict traitors without trial and the second bill sanctioned the arrest of those same suspects without trial.

Refusing to obey such subversive laws, Gandhi said, these bills were "evidence of determined policy of repression." He returned to active protests, joined the Home Rule League and also agreed to head the Khilafat Committee.

But it was the Jallianwala Bagh event that finally pushed him into politics. He discussed a mass movement with his peers. The name "boycott" was suggested but Gandhi chose to go with the phrase: Non-Cooperation. Even as he proposed the movement to support Khilafat at the Amritsar Congress, the much-awaited Montagu-Chelmsford Reforms were declared.

A NEW CONSTITUTION

The Government of India Act, 1919, became the new Constitution of India on 9th February 1921. This new system was called diarchy by the British; monarchy being the rule of one and diarchy being the rule of two: Britain and India. It introduced changes in provincial administration. According to this Act, the elected members set up two legislatures at the Centre – the First House was called the "Legislative Assembly" and the other "Council of State", which consisted of 33 elected members and 27 nominated members. Governors were appointed for major territories such as Bombay, Madras, Calcutta and Delhi.

The Governor-General had the right to summon, prorogue or dissolve chambers. He was empowered to prevent consideration of any bill or enact laws for the "safety, tranquility or interest of British Government".

The Central Legislature could make laws for entire British India but issues of defence, foreign policy and finance were the domain of the British government. Indian Legislature was given no powers on these subjects. In the central budget, certain items were open to discussion, but members had no right to vote.

The Provincial Legislative Council was expanded considerably. However, the bills passed by the Provincial Council required the assent not only of the Governor, but also the Governor-General. Both Muslim and Sikh electorates were given reserved seats in the Legislative Assembly and Legislative Council.

When the British King issued an appeal to the Indian people for cooperation with the new Constitution, Tilak immediately assured "responsive cooperation". However, at the annual session of the Congress, C.R. Das moved a resolution quite contrary to cooperation. He explained that these Constitutional reforms indicated that India was incapable of running a responsible government.

"Inadequate, unsatisfactory and disappointing,"

C.R. Das, speaking about the new Constitutional reforms

It was on this occasion that Gandhi took a leading role in the discussions. While Das rejected the reforms, Tilak favoured responsive cooperation with a view to prove British inadequacy. Gandhi advocated a trust in the British and pleaded with people to cooperate.

"To trust is a virtue," he said. "It is weakness that begets distrust." He believed that if something was accepted, it had to be done completely without any reservations. His sensible outlook received a great deal of support.

Though comparatively new in the Congress, Gandhi became the idol of many. However, he did not want to sideline Tilak. During one of the sessions, he took off his home-spun headgear (which later became famous as the Gandhi cap) as a gesture to plead with Tilak to compromise.

Later, they passed a resolution offering thanks to Montague for the reforms and his efforts towards an agreement with Turkey. Accepting the compromise, Das made it quite clear that he was not opposed to cooperation if it helped in achieving an early responsible self-government.

GANDHI TAKES CENTRESTAGE

In April 1920, Gandhi was elected President of the Home Rule League. On 15th May, peace terms were offered to Turkey by the Allies. On the advice of Gandhi, the Khilafat Committee adopted non-cooperation as a step towards complete independence on 28th May. On the same day, the Jallianwala Bagh inquiry report was published. The contents of this report sent shockwaves across the country. The findings of the inquiry commission and the judicial report presented a contemptuous justification of General Dyer's actions and barbarous insensitivity towards the victims. It wrapped General Dyer's guilt in the shroud of noble sentiments of loyalty towards the British government. General Dyer was made to resign from active service, but Britain absolved him of all charges.

To top it all, English societies collected funds for General Dyer, in appreciation of his efforts in ensuring the security of the British people in India.

The All India Congress Committee, which met on 30th May at Benaras, voiced their protest against the lenient attitude of the British government towards General Dyer.

To add to the prevailing discontent, inflation caused by high post-war prices led to near starvation of Indians. Gandhi convinced the Congress party that the answer to the prevailing discontent lay in non-cooperation. A special session of the Congress was called to consider the strategy. As a first step towards non-cooperation, the Khilafat Committee organized a strike preceded by prayers and fasting on 1st August 1920. On the same day, Bal Gangadhar Tilak died after a brief illness.

With a heavy heart, the special session of Congress, presided over by Lala Lajpat Rai, was held in Calcutta on 4th September 1920. In view of the circumstances, establishment of Swaraj seemed to be the only means to vindicate national honour, by adopting the policy of progressive nonviolent non-cooperation. During the open session, C.R. Das, B.C. Pal, Madan Mohan Malviya, Mohammad Ali Jinnah and Annie Besant strongly opposed the policy of non-cooperation. On the other hand, Motilal Nehru was among those who offered their full support to Gandhi and his idea of non-cooperation.

After Tilak's demise, Gandhi became the undisputed leader of Indians. Gandhi's oratory enthralled the masses. With slogans of "Mahatma Gandhi ki Jai", the supporters exhibited their approval and affirmed faith in the new gospel. Soon, their enthusiasm and early success of the movement brought dissenting leaders back into the Congress fold. The Khilafat issue, anger against the Jallianwala Bagh tragedy, need for political freedom, combined with economic pressures due to unemployment among the middle classes led to a new path of struggle.

The idea of non-cooperation was firmly adopted in the successive session in Nagpur in December 1920. Some of the unwilling members decided to compromise and became part of the movement. At Nagpur, Gandhi made a promise to his people that if they truly adopted the policy of non-cooperation in a nonviolent manner, Swaraj could be achieved within twelve months.

Meanwhile, the Congress was reorganized on the basis of gradation of committees, from the village level to bigger areas like sub-divisions, talukas, districts, provinces and the All India Congress Committee.

NON-COOPERATION IN ACTION

The message of non-cooperation carried by Gandhi rang with such personal appeal that each individual was eager to get involved. The simplicity of this idea touched everyone. Non-cooperation meant peaceful resistance – the refusal to help the British in its exploitation of India.

In included the following actions:

- Renunciation of government titles.
- Boycott of government law courts and establishment of people's courts in aid of settlement of common disputes.
- Withdrawal of children from government and government-aided

schools and establishment of national schools.

- Non-payment of taxes.
- Picketing of liquor and foreign goods shops.
- Boycott of durbars and government functions.

On the constructive side of the non-cooperation programme, stress was laid on hand-spinning khadi, Hindu-Muslim unity and removal of untouchability among the Hindus.

The die was cast, and a novel struggle began. Thousands of students gave up their studies in British-funded schools and universities. Eminent lawyers like Motilal Nehru, Sardar Vallabhbhai Patel and C.R. Das gave up their lucrative law practices forever. Rabindranath Tagore renounced his Knighthood.

Cloth being manufactured at a British mill in England

"The time has come when badges of honour make our shame glaring in their incongruous context of humiliation. I for my part, wish to stand, shorn of all special distinctions, by the side of those of my countrymen, who for their so-called insignificance, are liable to suffer degradation not fit for human beings..."

Tagore, in his repudiation letter to Lord Chelmsford, 1919

Students, teachers and professionals went from village to village to spread the message of non-cooperation. For the first time, Congress reached out to the poor. To the villagers, non-cooperation meant non-payment of taxes and keeping away from liquor, from which the government derived huge revenue.

Gandhi toured the country tirelessly in extreme weather conditions, addressing mammoth meetings. At the very sight of their leader, the people would burst into applause. Acting on his advice to not use foreign cloth, people took out their imported clothes and threw the garments into a bonfire. Gandhi wrote about non-cooperation in his English newspaper *Young India* and Gujarati daily *Navjiwan*.

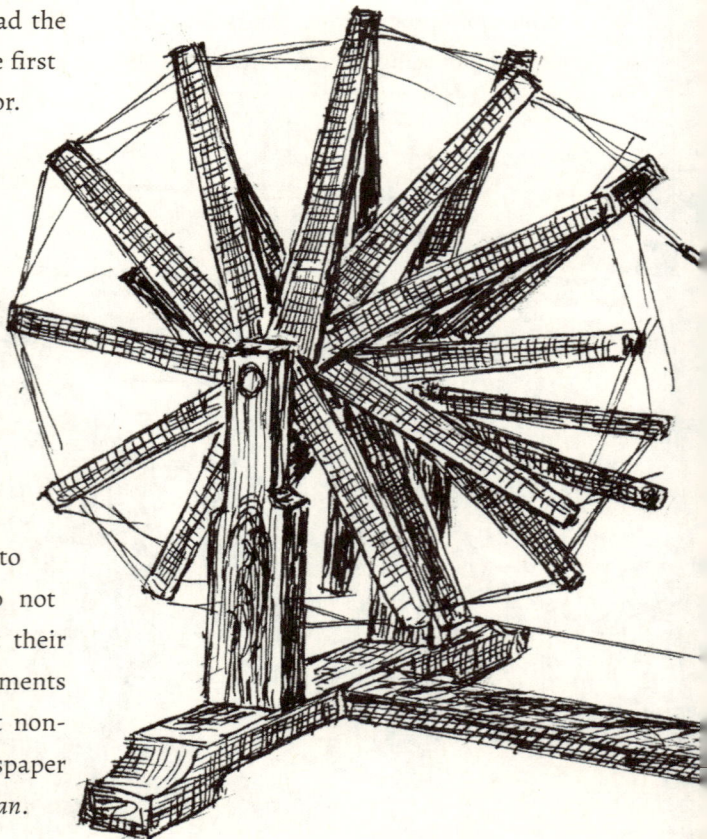

The most interesting aspect of the Non-Cooperation Movement was boycott of legislature, law courts, and government and government-aided educational institutions. At the All-India College Students' Conference, under the chairmanship of Lala Lajpat Rai, a resolution was passed to this effect. Consequently, a tremendous upheaval took place at these schools and colleges. The buildings of these educational institutions stood bare without pupils and teachers.

In Calcutta, B.C. Pal and C.R. Das led the students. Here, students picketed British-run and British-funded educational institutions to prevent others from joining them.

The boycott of the Legislative Councils proved to the world that the new Constitution did not represent the people of India. All Congress candidates withdrew from contesting the elections. Congress, in the words of American journalist Louis Fischer, was the "unofficial parliament in which all political trends and parties were or could be represented."

A more spectacular expression of boycott came forward during the royal visits of the Prince of Wales, and subsequently of King Edward VIII and the Duke of Windsor. In the true spirit of non-cooperation, the Congress Committee decided to boycott the royal event. On 17th November 1921, the Prince of Wales landed in Bombay, welcomed by a large number of ruling chiefs, leading businessmen and landed aristocrats.

An all out strike was announced by the leaders in Bombay. Huge crowds gathered at the beach for a boycott meeting being addressed by Gandhi. The flames of a bonfire lit the sky. In the excitement,

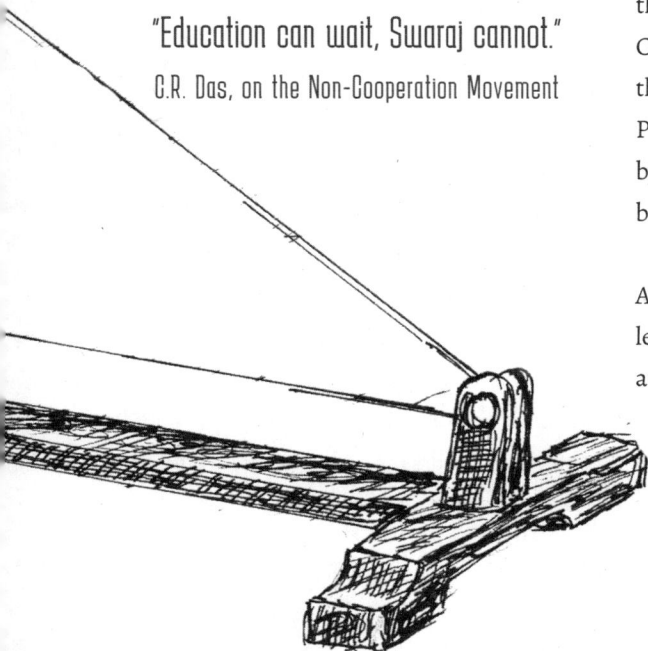

"Education can wait, Swaraj cannot."
C.R. Das, on the Non-Cooperation Movement

a section of the over-zealous crowd forcibly pulled the English hats of men and insulted Parsi women dressed in English attire. Similar hartals were observed in all the cities visited by the Prince, including Calcutta. Most of these hartals were peaceful, with the exception of Bombay.

> "A civilized form of warfare and yet dangerous to the stability of the state."
> Jawaharlal Nehru, describing the
> Non-Cooperation Movement

Non-cooperation was in effect "a peaceful rebellion". It inspired the masses to overcome their fear and express themselves freely. This renewed freedom of speech and action filled Indians with a sense of confidence and inner strength. Bitter feelings of communal hatred and discrimination between different castes and groups were washed away by the wave of nonviolent non-cooperation. The movement stressed on racial unity, communal harmony, promotion of swadeshi, especially khadi, and prohibition of alcoholic drinks.

The target set forth before the Congress by Gandhi was to collect one crore rupees for the Tilak Memorial Fund, enlist one crore members in the political party and arrange charkhas for twenty lakh households. In no time, this target was achieved due to the cooperation of the masses.

BRITISH TACTICS

As expected, the British government issued orders against public assemblies and processions, and declared the Congress and Khilafat organizations as unlawful for a period of three months in Calcutta and other major cities. Newspapers were banned and editors summoned for seditious writing, while leaders were summarily prosecuted for expressing dissent. An open war was declared by the government against non-cooperation. The British government justified its repressive measures by declaring that the intention of the movement was to paralyze the administration. British officers ordered their constables to beat and plunder (*maaro aur looto*). The Gurkhas broke loose in Chittagong. Indiscriminate arrests of Congress and Khilafat workers were made. People wearing Gandhi caps and khadi were singled out and insults were hurled at them.

In Calcutta, C.R. Das began to organize Civil Disobedience. Many leaders, including Das's wife Basanti Devi and their son, were imprisoned. British jails had lost their terror. Instead, imprisonment had become a certificate of distinction. As many as twenty-five thousand people were put behind bars, by the time the Congress Session took place. Many were shoved into police vans and left a few miles outside the city to walk back home. Tall leaders such as Motilal Nehru, C.R. Das, B.C. Pal, Lala Lajpat Rai, Mohammad Ali Jinnah and Gopabandhu Das were purposely given longer terms. Jawaharlal Nehru was sentenced to 18 months of rigorous imprisonment on charges of expressing his intention to picket foreign shops.

As always, British repression led to further discontent. The British government failed to realize that the nationwide revolt had its root in the demand for freedom. The British crackdown did not crush the revolt, and only widened the breach between Indians and their rulers. Even the moderates, now called liberals, vented open resentment and revulsion for the government.

The changed attitude of the moderates had a deep effect on Viceroy Lord Reading. He offered terms of reconciliation to Congress leader Madan Mohan Malviya, who had so far stayed distant from the movement. The Viceroy decided to lift the ban against all associations and passed orders to release all Congress volunteers. He also summoned a Round Table Conference of the representatives of Government of India and Congress to discuss the future Constitution of India. Malviya took charge and conferred with C.R. Das and Maulana Azad, who were in jail. Also known as Deshbandhu, Das exchanged letters with Gandhi to discuss the matter.

However, the Viceroy would not tolerate any delay. Much to the dismay of Malviya and Deshbandhu, the idea of the Round Table Conference was dropped.

MAPILLA REBELLION

While the spirit of nonviolence swept through India, an unfortunate incident by the Mapillas disturbed the harmony. The Mapillas – a Muslim community living in Malabar – were triggered into action with the stirring speeches of Mohammad Ali Jinnah. Swaraj, the oft-repeated catchword promising freedom from oppressive foreign rule, carried different meanings for different people and communities. For the poor harijans, it assured acceptance in society; for farmhands it meant a world free of landlord exploitation, and so on. The Mapillas understood Swaraj as an Islamic reign. When Jinnah was arrested, they broke into armed rebellion against the British government in the name of Islam. Some British officials fled to Calicut, but the remaining Europeans along with some Hindus were brutally murdered by the group. The Mapillas declared Swaraj and hoisted Khilafat flags.

But soon the rebellion was totally crushed and the English blamed Khilafat and non-cooperation movements for the revolt. The entire episode of violence pained Gandhi deeply. He strongly reiterated that the rebellion was a religious frenzy and not an off-shoot of the Non-Cooperation Movement.

The tide of the movement seemed to be receding, with most leaders in jail. Around the same time, the Khilafat issue became unimportant. Mustafa Kamal Pasha came to power in Turkey. The Caliphate was abolished and Turkey reorganized itself into a modern secular state.

Gandhi shifted his focus to villages. When the Congress met in Ahmedabad in December 1921, Gandhi announced his decision to resume the Civil Disobedience Movement, to address the grievances of farmers in Bardoli, a small tehsil in Surat. In his letter to the Viceroy, Gandhi sent an ultimatum.

"If the people join me, as I expect they will, the sufferings they will undergo, unless the British nation sooner retraces its steps, will be enough to melt the stoniest hearts."

Mahatma Gandhi, in his letter to the Viceroy

VIOLENCE AT CHAURI-CHAURA

Gandhi then proceeded to Bardoli. But the battle was lost before it even began. A dastardly crime was committed in Chauri-Chaura, a village in Gorakhpur, U.P. After a clash between peasants and the police on 5th February 1922, constables opened fire on the mob from their police station premises. However, once the ammunition was over, the cops locked themselves inside the building to save themselves from the angry mob waiting outside. The police station was set ablaze by the raging crowd, burning all policemen inside the building to death.

Before violence could spread, a disappointed Gandhi called off the Civil Disobedience Movement with immediate effect. The first phase of non-cooperation ended.

Soon after, on 18th March 1922, Gandhi was sentenced to a six-year imprisonment for his "seditious" speeches and writings, which "incited the public into violence".

To say that the Non-Cooperation Movement was a failure would be a mistake because it was successful in awakening the masses. Even to the uneducated lot, Swaraj was the sovereign remedy to all their problems. Thanks to the movement, Congress was turned into a real fighting force armed with the weapon of nonviolence. Due to the boycott, people conquered their fear of the British Raj. Men and women, rich and poor showed a willingness to endure hardships and suffer punishment. They fought social evils like drinking and untouchability through constructive programmes of the Congress. The practice of using charkha taught "bread labour" to the masses, as Gandhi called it. The emphasis on the use of khadi revealed a real understanding of rural needs and helped Gandhi win over the masses.

VIOLENCE PERSISTS

Hindu-Muslim relations suffered a huge blow after the suspension of the Civil Disobedience Movement. When the Movement was in full swing, both Hindus and Muslims looked at Swaraj from their own perspective. For Muslims, it was Khilafat; for Hindus, it was Hindu nationalism. The British government tried their best to defuse these forces by creating trouble within the two groups and encouraging violence. Such methods were the "stock-in-trade" of the imperialist government.

Another kind of nationalism also sprang up during this time. The Akalis formed an active, aggressive group among the Sikhs who were fighting for their religious beliefs. When the British unleashed their wrath on Sikhs by confiscating their sacred shrine at Guru ka Bagh, the Sikhs demonstrated extraordinary courage and bravery. In the true spirit of the creed of nonviolence, groups of Sikhs came one after another to face the sticks and batons of the police. Not one raised his hand. The Akalis won in the end and took possession of the shrine.

Nonviolence had stirred many groups. The majority of poor landless peasants and labourers, who were perpetually in conflict with their rich landlords, found a way to express their concerns, gaining greater confidence to walk side by side with their rich counterparts in the mass movement.

In trade, the malpractices of money lenders caused much anguish to the poor. In the villages, the condition of peasants grew worse, their debts increased, and to their dislike, the supremacy of the landlord and *sahukaar* prevailed.

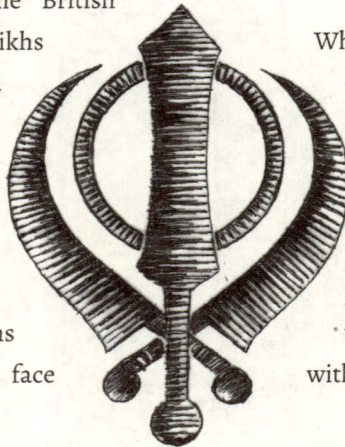

While these disruptive forces were at work, Gandhi was taken sick in Yervada Jail and had to undergo an operation. He was greatly disturbed by the communal trouble. Many "unity" conferences tried to bring about peace but without much success.

SWARAJ PARTY

A sense of disillusionment prevailed among the public. Under these circumstances, many questioned the efficacy of satyagraha. At this stage, leadership was provided by Motilal Nehru and C.R. Das. The Civil Disobedience Inquiry Committee reported that the country was not yet prepared for another mass movement. Motilal Nehru suggested that instead of boycotting the legislatures, non-cooperation should be carried out in the councils.

At the 1922 Congress Session in Gaya, Motilal Nehru declared that the Swaraj Party would demand the right of Indians to frame their own Constitution, and if denied, they would, in his own words, resort to a policy of "uniform, continuous and consistent obstruction with a view to make the government through the Assembly and councils impossible."

Prominent leaders like C. Rajagopalachari, Rajendra Prasad and Sardar Patel objected to it. Once again, Congress was divided, even though both factions maintained the same principles of nonviolence and non-cooperation. C.R. Das resigned and together with Vallabhbhai Patel, Madan Mohan Malviya and Mukund Ramrao Jayakar formed a new party known as the Congress Khilafat Swaraj Party. In the successive elections in November 1923, the Swaraj Party achieved remarkable success. It gained an absolute majority in Bengal, and became the largest party in UP and second largest in Assam. In the Central Legislative Assembly, the Swaraj Party formed a coalition with independents, moderates and the Muslim League headed by Jinnah, and formed the National Party. The joint party achieved remarkable success.

In 1923, T. Rangachariar appealed for self-governing Dominion Status within the British government and provincial autonomy in the provinces. Motilal Nehru exposed various fabricated charges against political prisoners in Bengal and requested for a Round Table Conference.

For the first time, national grievances were fully voiced, national aims freely expressed, exposing the ugly face of British policies in the legislature. The most outstanding achievement of the Swaraj Party was abolition of excise duty on cotton, import duty on sulphur, and the reduction of tax on salt. Unfortunately, the coalition of the National Party was soon divided on matters of budget, resulting in a walk out by leading Swaraj members before the term ended.

IDEOLOGIES AT PLAY

Meanwhile, within the Congress, differences of opinion was causing divisions. Lala Lajpat Rai and N.C. Kelkar formed a group of responsivists, those who offered cooperation to the British government. The other group, called the non-responsivists, included leaders like Motilal Nehru who withdrew from legislatures on account of their policy of non-cooperation with the British.

In June 1925, C.R. Das passed away, causing great loss to the cause. The position of the Congress was weakened by the growth of communalism. The Muslim League, which had remained inactive for four years, revived its programmes under the leadership of Jinnah. Madan Mohan Malviya regenerated the Hindu Mahasabha to promote the solidarity of Hindu organizations. Through non-Brahmin organizations, A. Ramaswamy Mudaliar advocated communal representation of non-Brahmins, Christians and Muslims in elected bodies of the government. The Communist Party began to organize working classes in unions, preparing for industrial and agrarian revolutions. However, the party was stopped in its tracks when the British government arrested its leaders.

Thus, began the famous Meerut Conspiracy Case in which the accused communist leaders won the sympathy of the people for their anti-British sentiments. Jawaharlal Nehru and Kailash Nath Katju became their defence counsel.

Meanwhile, opposing views were breaking the country apart. Communal riots broke out in Delhi, Allahabad, Jabalpur and Lucknow. Gandhi, who was released on grounds of poor health, tried to break the cycle of communal violence. He went on a twenty-one day fast as a penance for the inhumanity revealed in these riots.

In 1924, Gandhi became President of the Congress. Throughout the year, he toured the country, collecting funds for the political party. He urged more and more women to join the party, and made khadi mandatory for all Congress members. Spinning the charkha for at least half an hour a day became a regular activity for all party members.

KAKORI CONSPIRACY

In Britain, the conservatives came back to power in the Parliament. Lord Birkenhead, the Secretary of State for India, strongly opposed the proposal of allowing more reforms and Dominion Status to India.

This sent a wave of displeasure through the country and led to an increase in revolutionary activities in the country. A group of young energetic freedom fighters hatched a conspiracy for holding

up Number 8 Down train at Kakori, which carried the railway's daily earnings to Lucknow from Shahjanpur. The group included Ashfaqulla Khan, Rajendra Lahiri, Chandrashekhar Azad, Ram Prasad Bismil, Banwarilal, Manmathnath Gupta, Vishnu Sharan Dublish, and many others.

The sensational train hold-up at Kakori was the top headline in newspapers for the next few days. It resulted in a rough jolt to the British police. Many of the revolutionaries, including Ashfaqulla and Ram Prasad Bismil, were arrested and hanged to death. Poet turned revolutionary, Bismil famously defended his case in these words:

"Sarfaroshi ki tamanna ab hamaare dil mein hai. Dekhna hai zor kitna baazu-e-qaatil mein hai,"

Ram Prasad Bismil

REVIVAL OF NON-COOPERATION

The year 1927 suddenly brought a reason for the unity of all political parties. Lord Irwin succeeded Lord Reading as the new Viceroy. While Gandhi was touring in the south, Lord Irwin invited him for talks. Gandhi took the first train, travelling for two days and two nights to meet Lord Irwin at the appointed hour along with Vithalbhai Patel, Srinivasa Iyenger and Dr. M.A. Ansari – the President-elect of the Congress in 1928. Lord Irwin told Gandhi that a Commission to look into future reforms and structure of the government would soon be arriving in India from Britain. John Simon, Chairman of the Commission, would be accompanied by six members of the British Parliament.

According to the Government of India Act 1919, reforms needed to be reviewed from time to time, to modify or restrict the degree of responsible government. The Commission, which was to prepare the future Constitution of India, did not have a single Indian member.

Political parties, all unanimous in their view to boycott, received the findings of the Simon Commission with profound anger and condemnation. Thanks to the Simon Commission, the nationalist movement gained momentum, just as it had renewed itself in the past ahead of the royal visit of the Prince of Wales.

Meanwhile, the peasants' involvement in the struggle gathered fresh momentum. In Bombay, the peasants and workers forced the suspension of the Minimum Land Holding Act, which permitted increased landholding to prosperous farmers, by sidelining the poor.

Meanwhile, Jawaharlal Nehru led workers of the Kharagpur Locomotive Repair and Maintenance Workshop, in a strike against low wages and arbitrary company rules. However, the real upsurge of the movement took place in Bardoli.

BARDOLI SATYAGRAHA

For a long time, Gandhi had been waiting for the right opportunity to restart the nonviolent Civil Disobedience Movement. The stage was now set by the brewing unrest against the Simon Commission. Gandhi chose Bardoli to relaunch the movement, which had been shelved for six years. This time, the Civil Disobedience Movement was led by Sardar Vallabhbhai Patel and Abbas Tyabji. Gandhi watched from a distance.

On 12th February 1928, Patel began a satyagraha of peasants against a twenty-two percent increase in land revenue in Bardoli. The peasants refused to pay the taxes. As penalty, the collectors seized their cattle, carts, and lands, with an aim to auction these and recover the unpaid revenue. Many peasants and leaders were put behind bars. The agitation went on for months. The eyes of the entire nation were fixed on Bardoli. Moderates Sir Tej Bahadur Sapru and K.M. Munshi expressed their sympathy and complete support to the campaign. From all parts of the country, people urged Gandhi to make a formal announcement regarding the movement. But Gandhi patiently let the tempo build up.

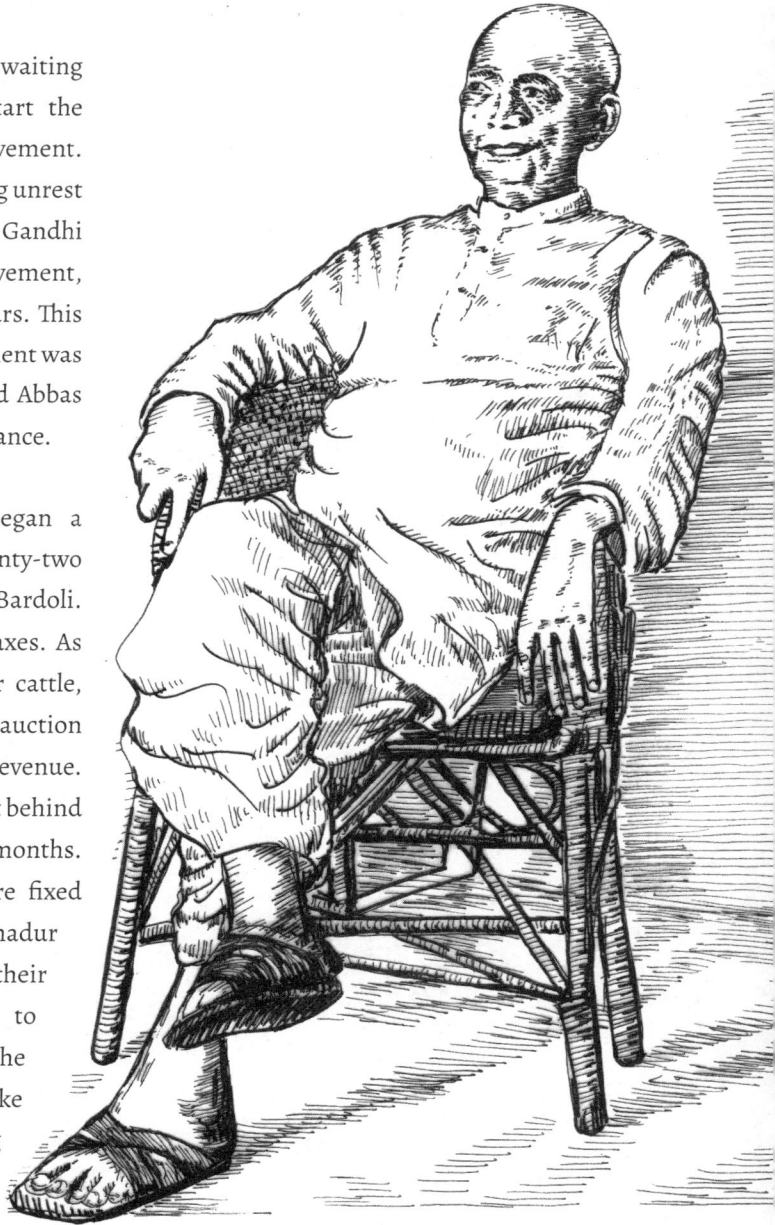

On 12th June 1928, the entire country joined in a peaceful hartal for Bardoli.

In August 1928, Patel was arrested by the British. Standing firm on their demands, the poor peasants refused to budge. The continuity of the agitation demonstrated the strength of nonviolence. Finally, the British government had to relent. It released all prisoners, returned confiscated property and cancelled the increase in taxes. The peasants paid the taxes at old rates, in keeping with their settlement.

The masses resolved to tread the thorny path of nonviolence with Gandhi, whose repeated insistence on refraining from violence and observing of fasts to atone for violent acts committed in the name of nonviolent non-cooperation had a profound effect on the people. They were ready to suffer but not yield; accept the blows but not strike back; stand steadfast in defence of truth but not give up the fight for their rights. They accepted the fact that a nonviolent movement was the only way to attain Swaraj.

SIMON COMMISSION

At the end of 1927, the Madras Congress Session was faced with vital issues. In response to the proposed boycott of the Simon Commission, Lord Birkenhead, Secretary of State for India, reminded the leaders of the challenge to draft a Constitution acceptable to all parties. The Congress accepted the challenge. The Muslim League and other parties approved.

Later, representatives of the All Parties Conference, met under the chairmanship of Dr. M.A. Ansari and dedicated themselves to this task. At the same session, Jawaharlal Nehru supported by Subhash Chandra Bose moved a resolution, declaring Purna Swaraj or complete independence as the ultimate objective of all Indians. Much more deliberation was given to the issue of immediate significance – boycott of the Simon Commission.

All political parties suggested measures to make the boycott effective. These included mass demonstrations, refusal to recognize legislatures and cooperate in the inquiry, and social boycott of the members of the Commission. Once again, all political differences were cemented. A new wave of mass resistance with greater enthusiasm than ever before swept through the country.

On 3rd February 1928, John Simon and his party touched the soil of Bombay, a city in the grip of hartal.

Also known as Salt Satyagraha, the march to Dandi inspired the whole nation to follow in the footsteps of Gandhi to demand freedom through peaceful resistance.

THE DANDI MARCH

1930 Dandi March • **1931** Lahore Conspiracy Case Executions
• **1931** Gandhi-Irwin Pact • **1931** Second Round Table Conference

"Simon, Go Back! Go Back, Simon!" A surging crowd greeted the Commission with this slogan. People waved black flags and organized protest marches all over the country. In Lahore, Lala Lajpat Rai, popularly known as Punjab Kesari (Lion of Punjab), led the procession on 30th October 1928. The peaceful march met severe opposition from the police, who brutally lathi-charged the protesters, using stout bamboo sticks with metal mounts. Lala Lajpat Rai was severely injured in the lathicharge, which led to his untimely death.

The Simon Commission was appointed to review reforms introduced by the Government of India Act, 1919. The Act had provision for a review after every ten years. In the past, many political parties had demanded the revision of these reforms to move closer to responsible government. However, the British had resisted any review. This is the reason why many were surprised when the government announced the appointment of a panel, comprising of seven parliamentarians, to review constitutional reforms. On 8th November 1927, almost two years before the completion of the ten-year period, Sir John Simon arrived in Bombay along with six other members of the British Parliament.

The hurried step was taken ahead of the General Elections in Britain in 1929. Britain's Labour Party, believed to be more sympathetic to Indian aspirations, was projected to come into power. In order to avoid any concessions to India, the Conservative Party-led government hastened the review by appointing the Simon Commission. Refusing to be fooled by the cunning move, Indian parties decided to boycott the commission on the following grounds:

Firstly, no Indian was appointed as a member in the Commission. Secondly, it was long demanded by Indians that the Constitution of India should be written only by Indians and not by the British. Thirdly, it was obvious to Indians that the British considered it an insult to let their subjects evaluate and decide on their future.

LAHORE CONSPIRACY CASE

The news of Lala Lajpat Rai's death spread like wildfire. The nation was drowned in sorrow. British high-handedness had agitated the people, especially the younger generation. The angst of young revolutionaries was channelized by Chandra Shekhar Azad, under the banner of the Hindustan Socialist Republican Association.

Angered by the cruel lathi-charge on peaceful protesters and the death of Lala Lajpat Rai, two young revolutionaries, Bhagat Singh and Shivaram Rajguru, shot dead Assistant Superintendent of Police, John Saunders, in Lahore, and escaped. They were supported in this act by Sukhdev Thapar. Through their electrifying actions, the Hindustan Socialist Republican Association wanted to awaken people from their slumber.

On 8th April 1929, the President of the Central Assembly was to announce his ruling on the Public Safety Bill, which was drafted to control the Communist movement in India. Two young exponents of the revolutionary thought, Bhagat Singh and Batukeshwar Dutt, dropped two bombs on the floor of the assembly, within an interval of two seconds. The duo threw red pamphlets after firing a few shots in the air. The flyers declared that the bombs weren't aimed at killing people and were only used to draw attention. As soon as the two were finished making a point, Bhagat Singh and Batukeshwar Dutt willingly surrendered to the police, shouting "Inquilab Zindabad" (Long Live Revolution), which became a war cry for India's freedom struggle.

"Inquilab Zindabad"

A series of cases slapped against these revolutionaries came to be known as the Lahore Conspiracy Case. While in Lahore jail, the young revolutionaries went on a hunger strike against the ill-treatment of Indian inmates. They demanded to be treated the same way as European prisoners. On a hunger strike for 63 days, the young Jatindra Nath Das died fighting for the cause. The tragic death had a deep impact on the nation. Thousands of people joined his funeral procession in Lahore.

Meanwhile, the farce of special tribunal was enacted and Bhagat Singh, Shivaram Rajguru and Sukhdev Thapar were sentenced to death on 23rd March 1931.

THE PLEDGE OF PURNA SWARAJ

In the meantime, political activity also gained some momentum. The boycott of Simon Commission had necessitated an alternative arrangement for framing the Constitution of India.

The Congress appointed its own Committee under the chairmanship of Pandit Motilal Nehru to frame the Constitution of India, which made it clear that complete independence was the only goal of Indians. However, the British were not yet ready to consider the demand for complete independence. Therefore, Gandhi suggested a compromise – Dominion Status, in return for the British approval of a Constitution drafted by the Congress Committee. Dominion Status meant that Indians would govern the country but the overall control would still be with the British government. In other words, the King of England would remain the Emperor of India.

Congress gave the British government a deadline of 31st December 1929, to take a decision on this compromise. When the moment arrived, there was no response from the British government.

As chilly winds blew on the night of 31st December 1929, a large crowd gathered on the banks of river Ravi in Lahore. The euphoric moment was joined by Congress president Jawaharlal Nehru. At the stroke of midnight, Nehru hoisted the tricolour flag of India. The wait was over, India was now free to demand Purna Swaraj (complete independence). The ecstatic crowd danced in joy, shouting slogans of "Bharat Mata Ki Jai". It was a moment everyone had been waiting for. The symbolic act kindled hopes of a glorious future for India.

On 26th January 1930, India took the pledge of Purna Swaraj under the leadership of Jawaharlal Nehru. To achieve this goal, Congressmen decided to boycott Legislative Councils. It was also agreed that the unjust laws will have to be defied through civil disobedience.

DANDI MARCH

The pertinent question was how to violate
the civil laws in a peaceful manner.
Gandhi spent days meditating in order to
devise a strategy to avoid violence
at all costs.

**People marching from
Sabarmati to Dandi**

monopoly over the commodity.

Gandhi decided to begin with the violation of salt laws. For this, he selected a place called Dandi near his birthplace Porbandar in Gujarat. The historic march from Sabarmati to Dandi spanned nearly 200 kilometres. More and more people joined him on his way to Dandi. The long distance and other agonies of the march did not deter the spirit and morale of Indians. Every new day that dawned intensified the will of the people, strengthening their determination. The march was reported all over the world through newspapers and radio, giving Gandhi yet another name – "Mr. Walker". The epic march awakened the people and gave them the courage to face a mighty force with love and compassion. Gandhi and his followers reached Dandi on 5th April 1930.

One day, while watching the sea waves lost in thought, Gandhi heard his "inner voice". A new idea came to him in a dramatic moment. Gandhi had been looking for an unjust law that affected all Indians. The 1882 Salt Act was one such law. Poor and rich, young and old, men and women, all needed salt to survive. But the Salt Law did not allow people to make salt, giving the British government a complete

On 6th April, Gandhi said his prayers and walked to the seashore. As a gesture to flag off the movement, he picked up a fistful of salt, breaking the law, as Indians and foreigners watched in awe. Gandhi believed that like other gifts of nature such as air and water, salt should not be taxed.

Salt pans

Thousands and thousands all over the country followed his action. Just as groups or *jathas* of Sikhs had followed one another during the protest against Guru Ka Bagh occupation, batches after batches of people came forward to collect salt on the seashore, as an act of satyagraha against the Salt Laws.

The women of India did not lag behind either. They responded to the appeal of Gandhi to take up the work of picketing and spinning. Many women discarded their purdahs and came out in full support. They joined the jathas raiding salt depots and did not flinch an inch even while facing lathis.

Sarojini Naidu (1879-1949), also called the Nightingale of India, had the distinction of being the first Indian woman President of Congress (1925). Naidu directed these raids at salt depots in Dharsana and assumed leadership after Gandhi and

Abbas Tyabji were arrested. She stirred the masses with her powerful oratory. "In the battle for liberty, fear is one unforgivable treachery and despair, the one unforgivable sin," she told the masses, expressing her frustration over the subjugation of Indians by the British.

"Behold! I rise to meet the destined spring,
And scale the stars upon my broken wing!"
Sarojini Naidu, *The Broken Wing*, 1917

From her commanding position, she reminded the picketers, "Gandhi's body is in jail but his soul is with you... You must not use violence under any circumstances. You will be beaten but you must not resist; you must not even raise a hand to ward off blows." One batch after another stepped forward to face the raining lathis. However, the police brutality persisted, as one lot fell the other took its place. At the salt pans of Dharsana, Naidu was arrested but continued to fight for the cause. Among other women stepping forward to take part was Kamladevi Chattopadhyay, who led salt satyagrahis at another location.

The participation of women was so significant that Jawaharlal Nehru was moved to describe it thus, "Our women came to the front and took charge of the struggle. Women had always been there of course, but now there was an avalanche of them, which took not only the British Government but their own menfolk by surprise."

The tremendous impact of this historic march and nationwide response to civil disobedience alarmed the British government. They passed an emergency ordinance and re-imposed the Press Ordinance once again. Under this, newspapers were fined for publishing about the Civil Disobedience Movement, and harsh measures were undertaken to suppress the movement.

Once again, the British government declared the Congress an unlawful organization and confiscated its property. But these repressive laws did not demoralize people, nor did it paralyse the Civil Disobedience Movement.

As the days passed, it continued to gain in strength. People refused to pay taxes. Peaceful volunteers picketed foreign goods shops. The police acted violently even when people were expressing themselves in a peaceful manner. They lathi-charged peaceful processions, fired at men, women and even children. When Gurkha troops refused to fire on peaceful satyagrahis, they were punished and court-martialled. More than 75,000 satyagrahis were arrested, filling the jails, where they were tortured by the British.

This way of fighting physical brutality with nonviolent resistance was a novel philosophy. The moral courage of ordinary people inspired by Gandhi was highly appreciated and admired all over the world. The injustice, witnessed and reported by foreign correspondents, lowered the prestige of the British government in other countries. But it had no effect on the perpetrator.

TOWARDS RESPONSIBLE GOVERNMENT

Even as the whole nation was in turmoil due to the Civil Disobedience Movement, the Simon Commission went ahead and submitted its report on 7th June 1930.

It recommended the following:

1. Provincial dyarchy should be abolished and responsibilities of ministers to the provincial legislatures should be enlarged.

2. The special power for the safeguarding of province and the protection of minorities comes under the Governor's powers.

3. The representation of provinces and other areas constituted on the basis of population at the Federal Assembly (at the Centre).

4. Recommended Dominion Status for Burma and should be provided its own Constitution.

5. Recommended the representation of Council of State could not be chosen on the basis of Direct Election but by Indirect Election through Provincial Council which is more or less just like modern-day election procedure of Proportional Representation.

The Indian Legislative Assembly rejected the report since most Indian members were in jail due to their participation in the Civil Disobedience Movement. Even the Liberal Party demanded that these recommendations should not form the basis of the Round Table Conference.

In spite of the opposition to recommendations of the Simon Commission, the British government went ahead with the First Round Table Conference in London in November 1930, without a single Congress member attending the conference. However, some important leaders like Tej Bahadur Sapru and Mohammad Ali Jinnah, and few princes agreed to attend it.

Everyone agreed that India should have elected governments at the Centre and in States. Indian people should elect their own representatives to make laws for India. In other words, India should have a Parliamentary system of government. Defence and foreign affairs should be reserved for the Governor-General with necessary administrative powers. Minority communities like Muslims, Christians and Sikhs asked for separate seats for themselves in the Assembly. Dr. B.R. Ambedkar also demanded that Harijans should be considered a separate community and not labelled as part of the Hindu community. The delegates felt that these differences over the representation to various minority communities could be sorted out later. Therefore, proceedings led by the Viceroy went one step further than the Simon Commission.

However, Congress, the largest party in India, had to approve these proposals before any concrete step could be taken towards a responsible government. For this reason, the British government released members of the Congress Committee on 26th January 1931.

But the Congress Working Committee did not react favourably as it felt that the Round Table Conference was not representative, citing the declaration of the British Prime Minister as "too vague and general to justify any change in the policy of Congress". To the Congress, the Round Table proposals were nothing short of a disappointment as they had been demanding for complete independence. The Congress then urged Gandhi to meet the Viceroy.

John Simon

GANDHI-IRWIN PACT

The marathon discussion between Irwin and Gandhi resulted in the Gandhi-Irwin Pact on 5th March 1931. The very word "pact" implied equality of status between Indians and the British Empire. The Pact laid out the following conditions:

1. Civil Disobedience Movement was to be called off.

2. Political prisoners were to be released.

3. Salt manufacture was to be permitted on the coast.

4. Congress would attend the Round Table Conference.

5. As per the Constitutional discussions, federal character of the Constitution was to be an essential part, and discussions could be undertaken in the interest of India in matters of defence, external affairs, minorities and financial credit.

Even though the pact was passed unanimously by the Congress on 6th March 1931, there was a lot of criticism against this settlement. Independence was not yet granted and even Dominion Status was not promised. According to the settlement, Gandhi called it "provisional" and "conditional", and a "truce". The goal remained, "complete independence" since "India cannot be satisfied with anything less," Gandhi declared before the Congress Working Committee. The Pact did not offer many political concessions, but it established equivalence of stature and cordial relations for the furtherance of responsible government.

"A politician would have sought more substance. Gandhi was satisfied with the essence: a basis for a new relationship."

Louis Fischer, *Mahatma Gandhi His Life and Times*, 1951

On 29th March 1931, the Congress members met in Karachi to approve the Gandhi-Irwin Pact. Gandhi's popularity reached its peak. As he himself remarked during the meeting, "Gandhi may die but Gandhism will live forever".

SECOND ROUND TABLE CONFERENCE

Gandhi sailed for London on 29th August 1931 along with Pandit Madan Mohan Malviya and Sarojini Naidu. This "Naked Fakir", as Churchill called him, won the hearts of all, right from the king to little children. Unfortunately, nothing much could be achieved during the Round Table Conference as the difference over communal awards persisted. The British policy of divide and rule prevented any agreement on communal award. As a result, no progress was made in the drafting of the Constitution of India and Gandhi returned disappointed.

In April 1931, Lord Linlithgow took over from Lord Irwin as the Viceroy of India. Unlike Lord Irwin, he was not very sympathetic to Indians. Viceroy Linlithgow did not look into the complaints against repressive officers. He also turned down the request of appointment of inquiry boards consisting of public representatives and official nominees. Nor was he in favour of a permanent Board of Arbitration to decide the question of interpretation of the Gandhi-Irwin Pact.

The Viceroy's attitude resulted in a tense political situation, which led to unrest in

Gandhi with Madan Mohan Malviya and A. Rangaswami Iyengar at the Second Round Table Conference

the United Provinces and Bengal. Khudai Khidmatgar, an outfit run under the leadership of Khan Abdul Gaffar Khan, in the North-West Frontier Province (NWFP), was declared illegal.

Gandhi, who had received news of these latest developments in London, dealt with the situation in his characteristic way as soon as he returned to India. He sent telegrams and letters to Viceroy Lord Linlithgow, complaining about repressive measures of the government and asked for a meeting. The Viceroy justified the actions of the British government and refused to meet Gandhi.

CIVIL DISOBEDIENCE

Civil disobedience was resumed with greater enthusiasm. Under Viceroy Linlithgow, the British government became much harsher. Important leaders were jailed. Young revolutionaries, who could not control their anger against police torture and harsh treatment given to peaceful protesters, were finding newer ways to express their discontent. They bombed important government buildings and tried to kill government officials and police officers.

One such important incident was the Chittagong armoury raid, where young revolutionaries tried to loot the Chittagong armoury in Bengal Presidency. Many of them, including women, were shot dead during the attack and the arrested were sent to *Kaala Paani*, the Cellular Jail in Andaman.

However, a majority of people were using peaceful ways to break British laws, in compliance with the Gandhi-led Civil Disobedience Movement.

All of a sudden, Gandhi put a brake to the movement on 8th May 1933. He wanted Hindus to treat the Harijans as their own people and not consider them as "untouchables" or low caste. Only then could they join in the freedom struggle. With the Civil Disobedience Movement coming to a halt, Gandhi wanted the

British government to free the satyagrahis. However, the then Viceroy Lord Willingdon refused to do so or even discuss the matter with Gandhi.

Again, Gandhi asked people to violate the laws in their individual capacity. Under the circumstances, he proclaimed, "every person to his own discretion" and conveyed to the leaders that each person was to offer satyagraha in their individual capacity. This was called vyaktigat satyagraha (Individual Civil Disobedience).

Gandhi was soon arrested on 1st August 1933. Nehru, Patel and other leaders were also taken into custody. When Gandhi was refused permission to conduct the untouchability campaign from jail, he decided to fast for 21 days. On 23rd August, he was released from prison due to his serious medical condition. The individual Civil Disobedience Movement was finally withdrawn in May 1934.

During this period, the Third Round Table Conference took place without representatives from the Congress. The gathering issued a white paper, describing the postulates and procedures to introduce the parliamentary system in India. The Congress Working Committee discussed the white paper in June 1934. There were many differences on the point of "Communal Award". According to the Communal Award, minority communities were given more seats than their numbers justified. The Congress Working Committee rejected these proposals and wanted the members to be elected by the people. It maintained that special representation be given to a major minority community.

Some members like Annie Besant and Madan Mohan Malviya, who did not agree to this approach by the Congress, left the party in October 1934. A disappointed Gandhi also announced his resignation from the Congress in October 1934. The political party, however, continued to look up to him for guidance. Soon, elections to the Legislative Assembly followed, making Congress the largest party and Jawaharlal Nehru an emerging leader.

THE TORCHBEARER

1929 Jawaharlal Nehru Becomes Congress President • **1931** Death of Motilal Nehru • **1936** Death of Kamala Nehru

Rising under the mentorship of Mahatma Gandhi, Nehru became a charismatic, radical leader whose ideas also shaped post-independence India.

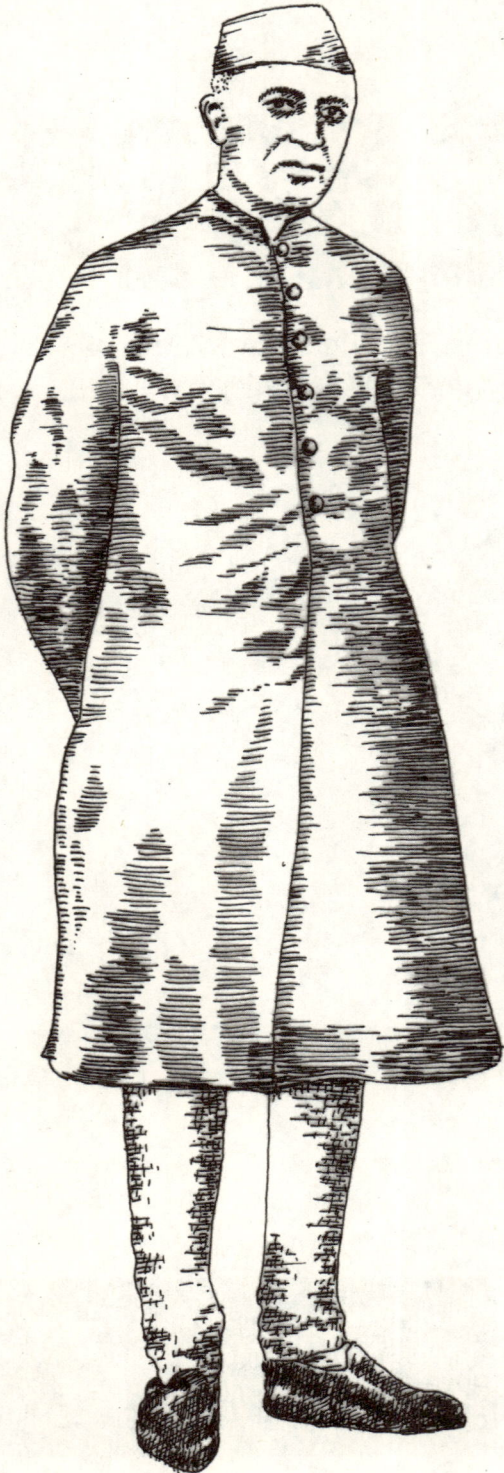

Jawaharlal Nehru was born on 14th November 1889, in Allahabad. Born of Kashmiri parents, Jawaharlal had two sisters. His father Motilal Nehru was a leading advocate of the Allahabad High Court and enjoyed a lavish lifestyle. Jawaharlal's mother Swarup Rani was a religious woman. After his early education at home by the best of tutors, he went to Harrow Public School in London. He was very fond of reading and his father's involvement in the Congress made him interested in politics from an early age.

Jawaharlal joined the Trinity College of Cambridge after finishing his schooling. During his college days, he not only read books on different subjects and browsed through every available newspaper but also attended lectures of well-known authors and political leaders like George Bernard Shaw and Lala Lajpat Rai. After getting a degree in Life Sciences, he joined the Inner Temple to pursue law. In the summer of 1912, he was called to the Bar, and soon returned to India to join his father's law practice.

However, the law courts did not offer much excitement to him. A great admirer of Bal Gangadhar Tilak, Jawaharlal studied the pulse of the people and realised the unjustness of the British Raj.

In the Congress sessions, the leaders, too, were giving vent to similar feelings, although in a moderate tone. During one such session attended by Jawaharlal, he got the feeling that it was an "English-knowing upper-class affair".

Jawaharlal was further drawn towards the politics of Bal Gangadhar Tilak, who had gained great popularity after his release from prison. During the Lucknow Session of 1916, a fiery speech made by Sarojini

Naidu also shaped his worldview. Young and full of energy, he did not like the moderate politics of the then Congress and his father Motilal Nehru.

Jawaharlal gravitated towards Gandhi's weapon of satyagraha, which was meant to rid people from fear of authority and imprisonment. Jawaharlal did not believe in the passive methods of moderate politicians. In contrast, his father Motilal was a firm moderate who believed that courting arrest did not serve any purpose. Young Jawaharlal was unwavering, and the morale boost he needed came from his wife Kamala who supported him. Eventually, Motilal Nehru came round to accepting his son's views following the dastardly attack on innocent Indians at Jallianwala Bagh.

At the end of 1919, the Congress session was held in Amritsar, where Motilal Nehru became the new President of the party. Around the same time, Gandhi was convincing people not to cooperate with the British government as part of the Non-Cooperation Movement, which was launched on 1st August 1920.

> Jawaharlal was restless. The British government, which had promised liberal concessions to Indians after the war, refused to stick to their word and instead imposed harsher laws like the Rowlatt Act.

As a first step in understanding the ground reality of British rule, Jawaharlal set out to meet the farmers and peasants of Allahabad. The farmers toiled hard to grow their crop but the grain was taken away by the *zamindars*, leaving the farmers in a hand-to-mouth state. Jawaharlal was so distraught by their poverty and helplessness that he decided to tour other villages in Uttar Pradesh. He was surprised to see how well the farmers were carrying out a peaceful satyagraha. As his admiration for Gandhi grew further, he decided to adopt Gandhism and support him in his endeavour. Jawaharlal started taking active part in Indian politics and took on the responsibility of spreading the message of peaceful non-cooperation in the villages of U.P. This was the beginning of a novel romance between him and the crowds.

After being disillusioned with the moderate approach, Motilal Nehru also joined Gandhi's Non-Cooperation Movement and gave up his lavish lifestyle.

During the visit of Prince of Wales to Allahabad, Motilal Nehru and Jawaharlal took the lead in boycotting the royal visit. Both father and son were arrested and sent to jail for six months, and a fine of rupees 500 was imposed. When they refused to pay the fine, the police entered their house, "Anand Bhawan", and took valuable items such as furniture and carpets, and threw out precious articles. The police did not treat the womenfolk with respect and reportedly manhandled Jawaharlal's mother.

This angered the people of Allahabad. Following the incident at Anand Bhawan, several volunteers came forward to take part in the protest.

In jail, Jawaharlal spun khadi on the charkha and taught prisoners to read and write. When Gandhi announced the withdrawal of the Non-Cooperation Movement after the Chauri-Chaura incident, Jawaharlal did not approve of the decision. Before Nehru could meet Gandhi, the latter got arrested by the British. Jawaharlal returned to Allahabad and organized people for picketing foreign goods shops. For this, he was arrested again and sentenced to one and a half years of rigorous imprisonment.

As soon as he was released, Jawaharlal left for Nabha in Punjab where Sikhs were agitating due to the overthrow of their king by the British. However, Jawaharlal was arrested at the border and put in a solitary cell. After a few days, he was set free and sent away from Nabha.

In 1925, his wife Kamala Nehru became very ill. Jawaharlal took her to Switzerland for treatment. While in Europe, he attended the Congress of Oppressed Nations at Brussels in 1927, where he represented the Indian Congress. Making full use of the opportunity, he met many international leaders like Ho Chi Minh and Madame Chiang Kai-shek and gained sympathy and understanding for the Indian cause. He apprised the world leaders of India's efforts to free herself from the oppressive British regime. During his stay in Europe, Jawaharlal read books on socialist philosophy and thought. His visit to Moscow strengthened his belief in socialism. While in Russia, Jawaharlal and Motilal Nehru heard about the appointment of the Simon Commission and immediately returned to India.

In Lucknow, Jawaharlal led a protest procession against the Simon Commission, where all of a sudden, the police resorted to a lathi-charge. The cops mercilessly thrashed the peaceful volunteers. Jawaharlal also received many blows. It infuriated him but he remembered Gandhi's teachings – "Violence always begets violence". Nonviolence is the only weapon to solve any problem. A true Satyagrahi must use the weapon of nonviolence and bear the bullets without protest. His grip loosened and he marshalled all his courage to bear the hard blows. He was hit hard on the head and almost fainted. Govind Ballabh Pant, another activist present there, rushed towards him to provide cover. Pant saved Jawaharlal from the thrashing, receiving all the blows on his own body. As a result of the injury, Pant's neck became unsteady for the rest of his life. Gandhi praised Jawaharlal and Pant for their courage and for being true satyagrahis.

In 1929, Jawaharlal succeeded his father and became the President of the Congress. Under his leadership, the pledge of Purna Swaraj was taken on the banks of river Ravi in Lahore, which was later ratified on

26th January 1930, promising people that India will become an independent republic one day.

When Gandhi's historic Dandi March resumed the Civil Disobedience Movement in the country, Motilal Nehru donated their home, Anand Bhawan, to the Congress and joined the movement along with Jawaharlal. Both father and son were arrested and sent to the same jail.

Kamala Nehru, who joined the Movement in spite of her failing health, also got arrested. Their daughter Indira organized a "Vanar Sena" of children and helped in carrying secret messages to and fro for the Congressmen. Motilal Nehru was released from jail when his health deteriorated, which ultimately led to his death in February 1931.

Throughout 1932 and 1933, Jawaharlal was mostly in jail, where he engaged himself in reading about world politics and economic systems.

His vision of a future India began to take shape. He dreamt of an India where all would be equal, everyone would have jobs and there would be no feuds between classes, castes and religions. He envisioned India as an economically and morally strong nation, which could take its rightful place in the community of nations. For this, a strong foundation of industrialization based on scientific outlook was needed. He considered dams, industries, power plants and research institutions to

be the temples of modern India. During this period, he wrote many books, including his autobiography *Glimpses of World History* – a collection of letters to his daughter, which became one of the most absorbing books on world history.

Jawaharlal was released in September 1933 after his mother became extremely ill. He started writing articles, criticizing the British government for inadequate relief for the victims of the Bihar earthquake and for the way the tragedy was handled by the authorities. The British government did not take kindly to the criticism and arrested Jawaharlal once again.

His wife Kamala did not have good health but had great courage. Jawaharlal was released in September 1935 when her condition became critical, and rushed to Switzerland to be with her. Kamala Nehru died on 28th February 1936. Following her untimely demise, Jawaharlal dedicated himself entirely to his work. The forthcoming elections provided an opportunity to channelize his boundless energy and organizational ability.

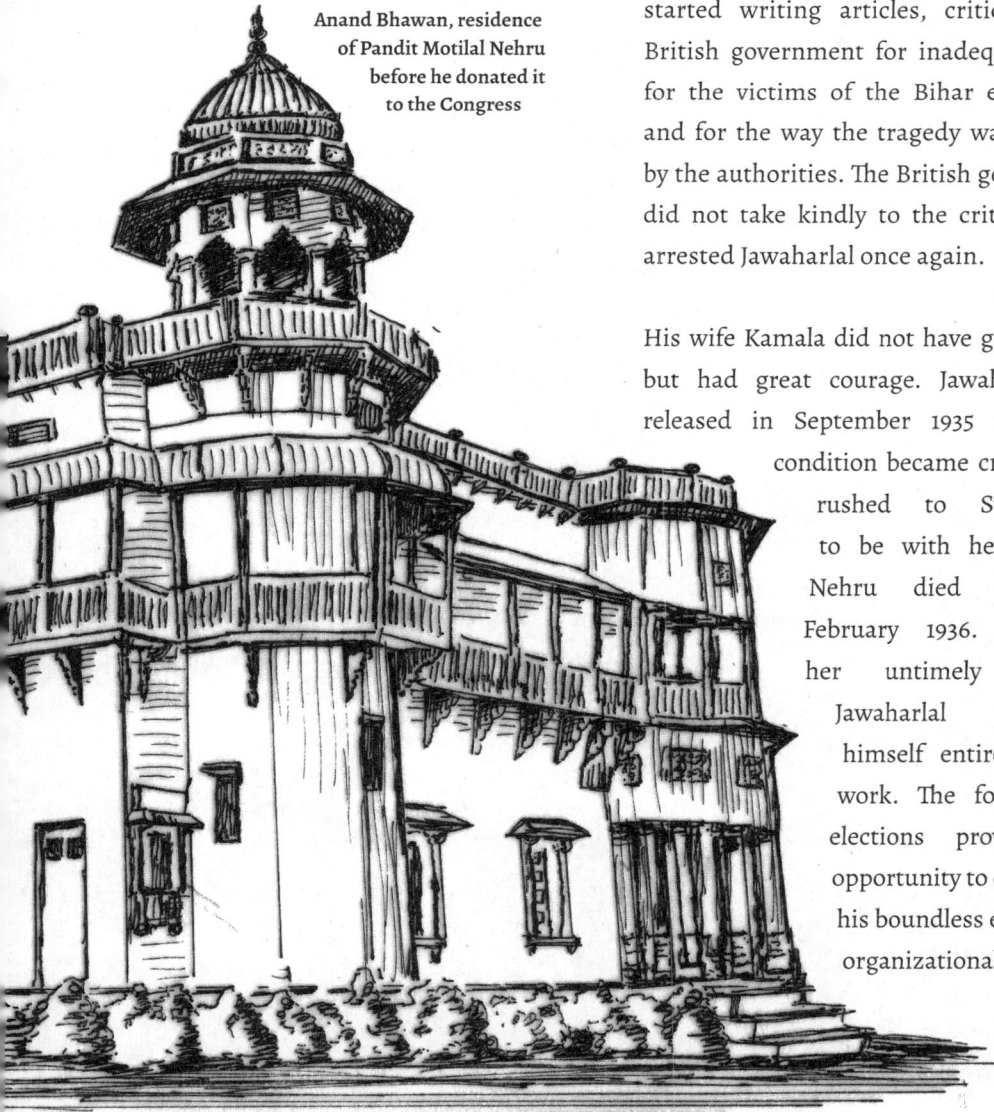

Anand Bhawan, residence of Pandit Motilal Nehru before he donated it to the Congress

The Second World War took the lives of 87,000 Indian soldiers, wounded nearly 35,000, and sent as many as 68,000 to prison.

THE SECOND WORLD WAR

1932 Third Round Table Conference • **1937** Indian Provincial Elections • **1938** Bose Becomes Congress President • **1939** Second World War Begins • **1943** Azad Hind Government

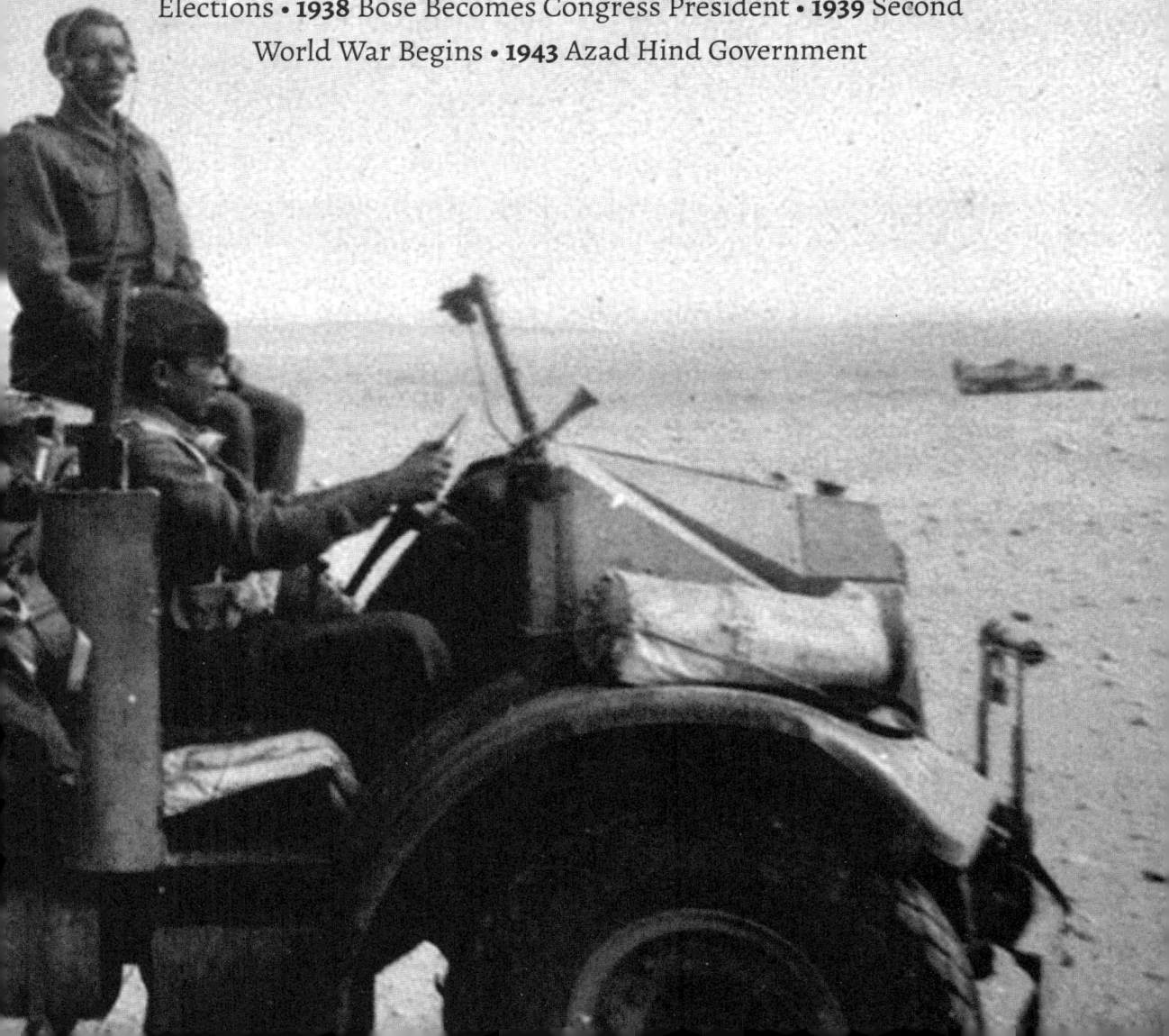

The Congress Committee did not agree to the proposals in the white paper, which were issued after the Third Round Table Conference in 1932. In spite of their displeasure, the British government went ahead and introduced a bill, known as the Government of India Act of 1935 on 19th December 1934. Even though Churchill opposed the bill, it was passed in the Parliament. Indian Provincial Elections under this Act were held in 1937. Congress chose to fight these elections even though the party had opposed the proposals in the first place.

Jawaharlal Nehru and other leaders toured all over India to gain support. In U.P., Rafi Ahmed Kidwai mobilized large funds for these elections. The Congress won a majority in the United Provinces, Madras, the Central Provinces, Bihar and Orissa, and emerged as the single largest party in Bombay, Bengal, Assam and North-West Frontier Province (NWFP). The Congress formed governments in these states and worked for the welfare of the people. Only in Sindh and Punjab it did not get a majority. There was no Congress Session in 1937 as the Congressmen were busy running the Provincial governments.

In 1938, at Haripura (Gujarat), Subhash Chandra Bose was unanimously elected as the Congress president. This gave a boost to radical elements in the Congress who had already organized themselves as a socialist wing within the party. Among this brand of leaders, Subhash Chandra Bose was the most popular.

When Second World War broke out in 1939, the Congress was heading the government in eight states. By 1938, the growing rift between radical forces and Gandhian Congressmen widened. The younger group, headed by Bose, wanted the Congress to take advantage of the war situation and start the Non-Cooperation Movement. In sharp contrast, Gandhi wanted to negotiate with the British regarding the demand for Independence.

Meanwhile, Bose and his colleagues, who believed in socialism, established a National Planning Committee for drawing up a plan for industrialization and economic development of the country. Again, Gandhi did not favour massive industrialization and wanted to focus on cottage industries. The differences between these two groups became more evident than ever in 1939.

In the same year, for the first time since 1907, elections for the Congress president were held. Maulana Azad, Subhash Chandra Bose and Sitaramaiyya were in the running. Maulana Azad withdrew his name. In spite of Gandhi's support to Sitaramaiyya, Bose won the election, proving his popularity. But the differences and discontent reached breaking point when thirteen members of the Working Committee resigned, leaving only two members in the fray – Subhash Chandra Bose and his brother Sarat Chandra Bose.

Another move was to put forward the resolution in AICC, directing the president to nominate working committee members as per the recommendations of Gandhi. After much confusion and adjournment, the resolution was passed and gave considerable powers to Gandhi but he refused to offer any suggestions to Bose regarding the working committee.

Thereupon, Bose resigned from the position of Congress President and Dr. Rajendra Prasad was elected in his place. He re-nominated the 13 members who had resigned when Bose was elected.

"If the rightwing really want national unity and solidarity,
they would be well advised to accept a leftist as president."
Subhash Chandra Bose, in a statement to Sardar Vallabhbhai Patel and the Congress, 1939

DR. RAJENDRA PRASAD

Hailing from Bihar, Dr. Rajendra Prasad was a bright and dedicated individual. A meritorious student, Prasad worked as a teacher in Bihar after completing his post-graduation in Calcutta. Later, he studied law and became an advocate. Prasad was drawn to the freedom struggle and joined Gandhi in the Champaran campaign, during which he pleaded cases on behalf of poor indigo peasants. His dedication and meticulous approach impressed Gandhi.

Affectionately called Rajen Babu, Prasad became the trusted soldier of the freedom struggle. He established the Sadaqat Ashram to inspire and motivate people to join the struggle and was imprisoned many times. In 1939, when he assumed presidentship of Congress, Britain declared war against Germany.

Dr. Rajendra Prasad

SUBHASH CHANDRA BOSE

Right from his student days, Subhash Chandra Bose showed leadership qualities. As a young student, he successfully organized a fast on the death anniversary of Khudiram Bose, a revolutionary who was hanged to death by the British government. Bose was expelled from college due to his role in organizing political strikes. He enrolled himself in the military training corps at the Scottish Church College, where he proved himself to be the best cadet and was given a captainship. He went to London to appear for the Indian Civil Service examination, where he stood fourth in the merit list and was immediately selected.

Interestingly, once his merit was proved, he refused to serve the imperialistic British government. His resignation created a stir in the government. After his return from England, Bose met Gandhi in Bombay, who advised him to meet Chittaranjan Das, popularly known as Deshbandhu, in Calcutta. Bose did so and became an instant admirer of Das, who was a lawyer and freedom fighter. Bose stayed on to carry out his activities in Bengal under Das's leadership.

In 1921, Bose was arrested for taking part in anti-government activities. This was followed by other jail terms for leading the Civil Disobedience Movement. In 1931, Bose was taken ill in jail and released by the government. After getting treatment in Europe and recovering from his illness, Bose toured many European countries to create awareness about India's freedom struggle.

Subhash Chandra Bose

He inspired young followers with his radical views, making him as popular as other tall leaders like Jawaharlal Nehru. Even though he was unanimously elected as the President of Congress in 1938 he was mostly supported by the youth and many senior Congressmen did not approve of his "militant" views. This led to a rift, which resulted in his resignation from the Congress to form a new party called the Forward Block. The new political party demanded immediate and complete independence from British rule. For this, the Forward Block organized their own civil disobedience movement, for which he was jailed. While in prison, he came to the conclusion that independence could be achieved only through military action. After being released from jail, Bose went on a hunger strike, for which he was punished with house arrest. Determined to pursue his goal, Bose decided to escape to some other country to run his freedom campaign.

THE FAMOUS ESCAPE

One day, a gentleman dressed in Muslim attire came out of the building where Bose was confined. He took a taxi to catch the first train to Peshawar. On reaching Peshawar, the man disappeared. In another part of the country, a physically challenged

Azad Hind Army

Pathan took on a journey from India to Afghanistan, in a truck carrying goods to Kabul. From here, the man set out for Germany's capital city Berlin via Moscow, and stunned the world by announcing his true identity.

No points for guessing that the impersonator was none other than Subhash Chandra Bose. As soon as the news reached the British government, they knew that Bose had tricked them. However, there was nothing they could do now to arrest him.

Even though both Bose and Germany were fighting a common enemy, that is the British, Germany was too distant from India to take up its cause. He then sailed to Japan, which was closer to India, and eventually went to Singapore, where he was welcomed by Rash Behari Bose and others. Here, he organized the Indian National Army, consisting of Indian soldiers captured by the Japanese during Second World War. He also raised a women's battalion and called it Rani of Jhansi Regiment.

Bose announced the formation of the Azad Hind Government on 21st October 1943. People from all walks of life contributed funds for his army. He joined hands with the Japanese forces and captured Kohima in March 1944, where the tricolour of India was hoisted. However, they could not move further as the British had a strong army in Imphal and the Japanese failed to send Bose the help they had promised. The arrival of rains made it even more difficult for the Azad Hind Army to move with their arsenal.

Bose advised his people to be brave even in their defeat. As the Second World War came to a close, Japan surrendered to the British and American troops. Azad Hind troops were also forced to give up their fight. Thus, once again, militant or violent methods proved unsuccessful to defeat British imperialism. To save him from falling into enemy hands, Bose's officers forced him to escape. His plane disappeared mysteriously, never to be found.

JAYAPRAKASH NARAYAN

The Congress Socialist Party was formed in 1934, with Acharya Narendra Dev as its President and Jayaprakash Narayan as its General Secretary. The Socialists believed that the State should provide every citizen with equal opportunities for self-development. There should be no bias on the basis of one's social status, and all citizens should have an equal share in the national wealth.

Born in village Sitab Diara located on the UP-Bihar border, Narayan was educated in Patna and received his higher education from universities in the USA. On return to India, he joined the freedom movement. While in jail for his activities, he met thinkers like Ram Manohar Lohia, Ashok Mehta, Minoo Masani and Achyut Patwardhan, who were trying to steer the Congress towards socialism. Narayan was jailed several times and, like Bose, succeeded in escaping from high security jails such as the one in Hazaribagh, Jharkhand. The British chased the fugitive from place to place until he was caught at last and jailed in Lahore, where he was tortured by the British. Narayan attained great popularity amongst the youth for his courage and daringness.

THE SECOND WORLD WAR AND INDIA

The Congress was dead against India's participation in Second World War. However, it failed to have a say in the matter due to a number of reasons. Even though the party had won elections in various provinces that agreed to go with the Congress stand, non-Congress provinces such as Punjab, Bengal and Sindh chose to extend their full support to the British. Many of these states were ruled by maharajas or princes, who declared their loyalty to the British by supporting the war efforts.

Political parties like the Hindu Mahasabha and the National Liberal Federation supported the government unconditionally. Similarly, the Muslim League did not prevent its ministers from supporting the government. Only the Congress refused to cooperate with the government.

"But India cannot associate herself in a war said to be for democratic freedom when that very freedom is denied to her."
Congress Working Committee Resolution, 1939

DOMINION STATUS

Viceroy Linlithgow declared that the British government might consider granting Dominion Status to India on conditions laid out in the Government of India Act, 1935. A new system of government was proposed by him, giving more autonomy to the Provinces of British India and a provision for the establishment of a Federation of India, which would comprise of British India and some or all princely states. Direct elections and reorganization of provinces was also suggested for India to rule under the umbrella of the British Empire.

To seek the cooperation of Indian people, the Viceroy wanted to establish consultative groups representing all political parties and princely states. Known as the "October Statement", the group was to be presided over by the Governor-General himself.

However, Congress refused to support the proposal as it could see through the rhetoric and considered Viceroy Linlithgow's declaration as the same old imperialist policy. As a symbol of protest, it called upon its ministries to tender their resignations between 27th October and 15th November 1939. In a way, these resignations made the task of the Viceroy easier as he was relieved of the task of convincing the Congress.

Nonetheless, as a last ditch effort, the Viceroy proposed more powers for Indians in the administration, but Congress did not yield. The party wanted the government to make a definite statement about granting independence to India by appointing a Constituent Assembly. However, Mohammad Ali Jinnah, president of the Muslim League, was opposed to the idea of appointing a Constituent Assembly as it would have more Congress members than the Muslim League.

Aware of Jinnah's stand, the Viceroy turned to the Muslim League.

Born in Karachi, Mohammad Ali Jinnah had his early education in Karachi and Bombay. At the age of 16, he sailed to England to study law. While in London, he was impressed by the liberal political thoughts of liberal statesmen such as William E. Gladstone, John Morley and Dadabhai Naoroji.

After completing Bar-at-Law, Jinnah returned to India in 1896 to practice law. He rose to fame as an expert lawyer and joined politics in 1906. Jinnah was elected to represent Muslims in the Viceroy's Executive Council in 1909 and enrolled himself as a member of the Muslim League in 1913.

DEMAND FOR PAKISTAN

Though Jinnah believed in Hindu-Muslim unity as a prerequisite to fight Britain, he insisted on special electorates and seats for the Muslims in the assembly. Jinnah believed in constitutional methods and therefore did not cooperate with Gandhi's method of non-cooperation or civil disobedience. He broke away from the Congress in 1928 and attended the first and second Round Table Conferences. During the Conference, he met Iqbal, a poet who was an advocate of a separate Muslim State. At that point, Jinnah differed with Iqbal and did not believe in a two-nation theory. He returned to India in 1935, when the Government of India Act 1935 came into being. The assembly elections were announced in the first week of 1937 and Jinnah decided to participate as a representative of the Muslim League.

The Congress victory in many states and the Muslim League's performance in Muslim-dominated areas led Jinnah to declare at the League's Session in Lucknow, "present Congress policy would result in communal war". This speech widened the rift between the Congress and the Muslim League. Supported by Liaquat Ali Khan, a Muslim philanthropist and political leader, Indian Muslims decided to put their weight behind Jinnah by the time the Second World War was declared.

On 22nd December 1939, the Muslim League observed a "day of deliverance and thanksgiving, as a mark of relief that the Congress regime has, at last, ceased to function". The final nail in the coffin came when during the Lahore Session of the Muslim League in 1940, the demand for a separate Muslim State was passed and the idea of Pakistan was born.

> "We stand unequivocally for the freedom of India. But it must be freedom of all India and not freedom of one section or, worse still, of the Congress caucus – and slavery of Mussalmans and other minorities."
>
> Mohammad Ali Jinnah at Lahore Session of the Muslim League, 1940

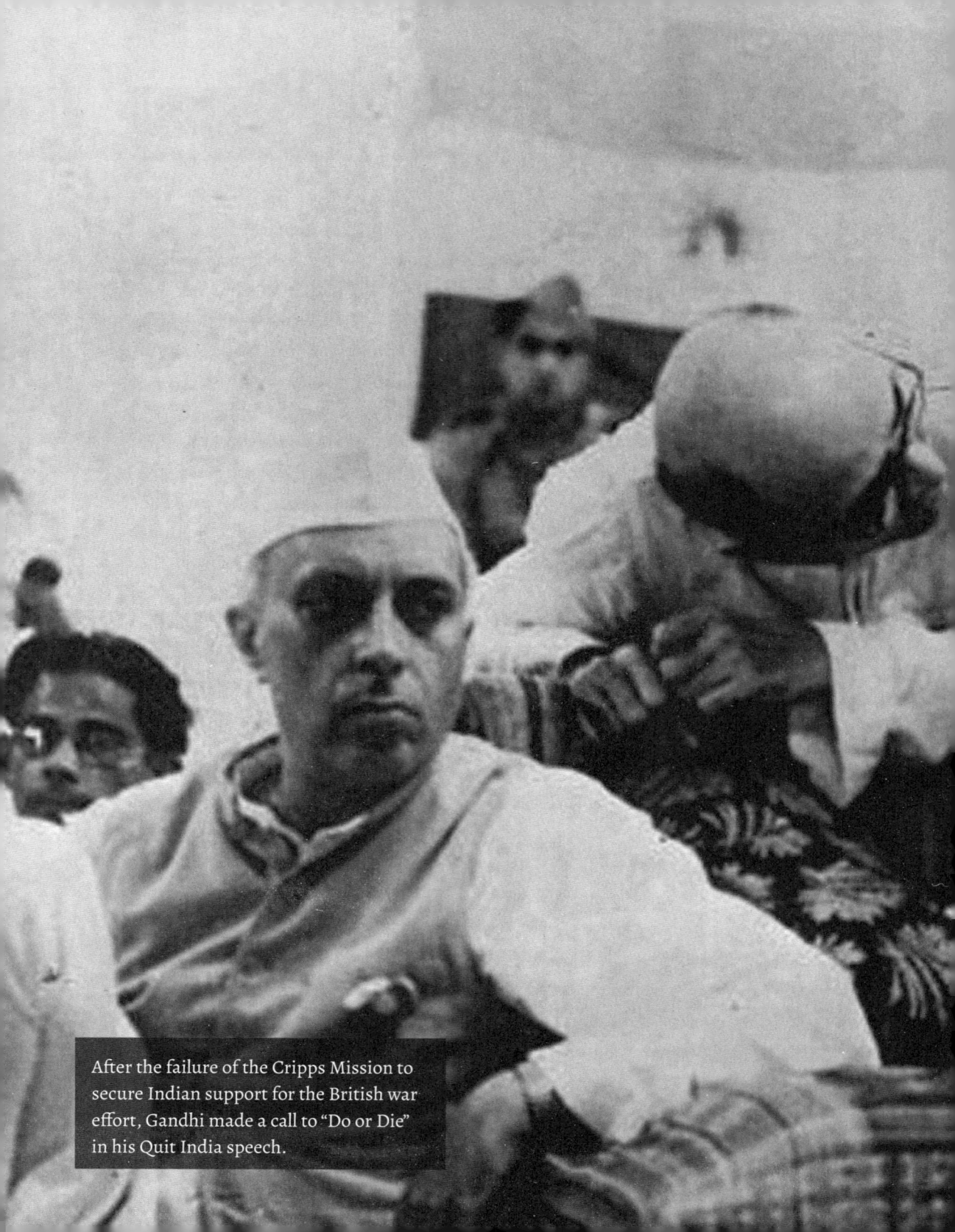

After the failure of the Cripps Mission to secure Indian support for the British war effort, Gandhi made a call to "Do or Die" in his Quit India speech.

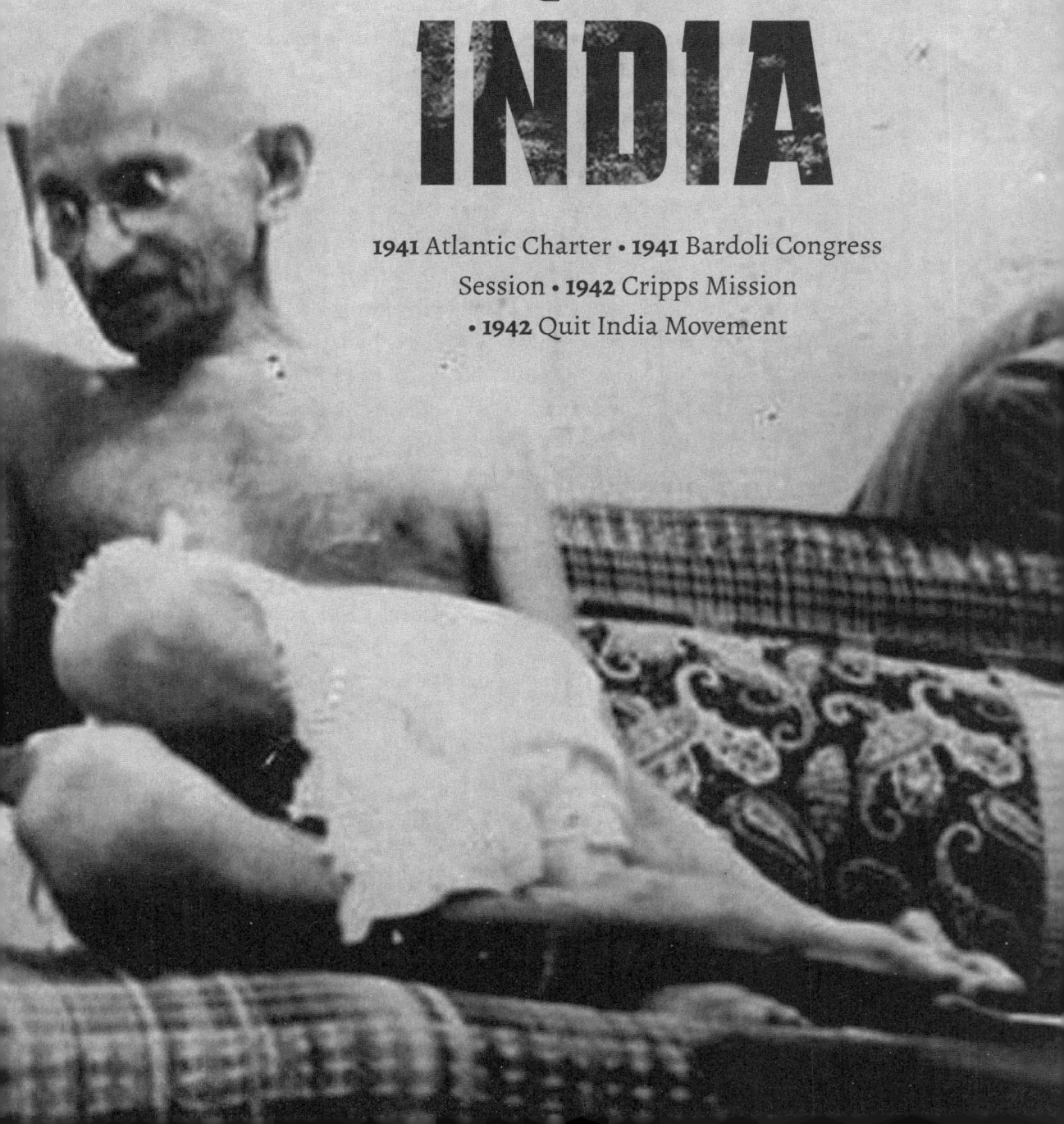

QUIT INDIA

1941 Atlantic Charter • **1941** Bardoli Congress Session • **1942** Cripps Mission • **1942** Quit India Movement

The Ramgarh Session of Congress, held in March 1940 under the presidentship of Maulana Abul Kalam Azad, declared that "nothing short of complete independence can be accepted by the people of India and they alone can shape their own Constitution".

The Congress also warned the government that it might resort to civil disobedience. Meanwhile, even before the Congress could organize itself to execute the campaign, the Forward Block, led by Subhash Chandra Bose, started its own Civil Disobedience Movement during the national week or "week of awakening" from 6th to 13th April, in 1940.

Gandhi was still confident that some understanding could be reached between the British government and the Congress. The Congress Working Committee met in Delhi from 3rd to 7th July and reiterated its demand of full independence for India. As a first step, the party wanted the government to constitute a National Government, which would have the support of elected members of the Central Legislature. In other words, the Congress was ready to take up administrative responsibilities and help war efforts of the government, provided the government made a firm commitment of complete independence after the war.

However, the Viceroy came up with another proposal, later known as the "August Offer". It stated that a representative Indian body could be formed to frame the constitution only after the Second World War was over. The offer also stated for the very first time that the Viceroy's Executive Council would be expanded to include more Indians than whites. However, defence, finance and home portfolios would remain with the British.

The Viceroy also declared that the British would not accept any system of Indian government whose authority was directly denied by powerful elements in India's national life. This pleased Jinnah and the Muslim League as it meant that without their consent, no government could be formed.

As expected, Congress rejected the offer. Meanwhile, the Civil Disobedience Movement launched by the Forward Block was in full swing. But Gandhi did not approve of the nationwide non-cooperation. He launched a new kind of individual satyagraha and representative satyagraha of selected groups. But the campaign did not receive the same response as it did during the Non-Cooperation Movement.

THE ATLANTIC CHARTER

A joint declaration issued on 14th August 1941 by America and Britain, the Atlantic Charter set out a vision for the postwar world. Among its major points was a nation's right to choose its own government. People around the world welcomed the move. But the British Parliament under Churchill declared that the Atlantic Charter did not apply to India. Thus, any hope of getting the commitment of independence from the British Parliament was once again dashed.

Meanwhile, Japan entered the war and captured Singapore. Even though the Japanese propagated the fact that they were coming to India to free her from British rule, hardly anyone in India bought the rhetoric. Jawaharlal Nehru, Maulana Abul Kalam Azad and other leaders, who were recently released from jail, made another appeal to the British for some understanding in the wake of Japan's aggressive posture but there was no change in the British policy.

At the Bardoli Congress Session in December 1941, the working committee decided to organize defence committees, on a national basis, to provide much-needed protection to Indians since war was on the doorstep of India. Meanwhile, the Muslim League was repeating its demand for Pakistan, while the Hindu Mahasabha countered this line of thinking with "Akhand Bharat" (undivided India) slogans.

In March, Burma succumbed to Japanese aggression. American President Franklin D. Roosevelt who was aware of the danger Japanese aggression posed to India, urged Churchill to settle the matter with India. As an ally of America, Britain agreed to send Sir Stafford Cripps to India.

THE CRIPPS COMMISSION

Sir Stafford Cripps arrived in Delhi on 23rd March 1942 and brought the following proposals for the Congress and the Muslim League.

1. For the earliest realization of self-government in India, steps would be taken to create a new Indian union with full Dominion Status.

2. Immediately after the war, a constitution-forming body would be set up. This body would be elected by the elected members of the Provincial Legislatures. Indian princely states would send their representative based on the population of their State.

3. British government would accept the Constitution thus framed on two conditions. Any province or provinces which were not prepared to accept the Constitution framed by the Constitution-making body could frame their own Constitution and be given the same status. Similarly, Indian states under princely rule would be free to accept or reject the Constitution framed by the body. In both cases, treaty arrangements would be negotiated.

4. The other condition was that the treaty signed between the British government and the constitution-making body must protect the rights of all races and religious minorities, as promised by the British.

5. Till the framing of the new Constitution, the British government would be responsible for the defence needs of India as a part of its war effort. The task of organizing materials, military personnel and other resources would be the responsibility of the Government of India, in cooperation with the people of India.

On the surface, these proposals fulfilled the demands of the Congress but in reality they pointed towards the partition of India. Secondly, the British left the choice of determining the future of those living in the princely states to their rulers.

For these reasons, the Congress Working Committee did not agree to the Cripps proposals. The Hindu Mahasabha also refused on the ground that it amounted to political division of India. The Muslim League was also dissatisfied as it felt that there was no definite announcement in favour of Partition. Even though "Pakistan is recognized by implication" but the party needed a clear commitment. Besides this, the depressed classes, Sikhs, Anglo-Indians and Indian Christians also demanded sufficient safeguards for themselves.

Another reason for the Congress disappointment with the Cripps proposal was that the defence forces were still under the control of the British.

The Congress was ready to reserve certain functions, which are to be carried out by the Commander-in-Chief during a war, but wanted all administrative functions, including defence, to be handed over to the National Government. It insisted on some modifications to the Cripps proposals. But the British government in England was not ready to give up any control as far as defence was concerned. Secondly, the National Government

envisaged by Cripps was nothing but the same Executive Council of the Governor-General. The British government was not ready to give the council full powers. In spite of the pressure put by the American president, the British government headed by Churchill stubbornly stuck to its stand. A failed mission, the Cripps Commission returned to London without achieving anything.

The people were growing more and more restless. Young Indians felt smothered due to inactivity in the political landscape. Gandhi, who could always read the sentiments of his fellow countrymen, expressed his unwillingness to wait any further. Gandhi wanted to revive the movement.

However, Jawaharlal Nehru and Maulana Azad felt that the time was not right as the Japanese were on the doorstep. But since the rest of the leaders were ready to back Gandhi, the Congress Working Committee passed the Quit India Resolution on 14th July 1942. It announced a nationwide nonviolent struggle led by Gandhi. As these steps would have far reaching consequences for the people of India and the world, the Working Committee decided to take the approval of the All India Congress Committee, which was going to meet on 7th August 1942, in Bombay.

Another compassionate friend of India, Miss Slade, named Mirabehn by Gandhi, went to Delhi to meet the Viceroy regarding the resolution. The Viceroy refused to see her and declared that the government "would not tolerate any rebellion during the war whether it was violent or nonviolent".

"I feel that I cannot afford to wait. If I continue to wait, I might have to wait till doomsday... That is why I have decided that even at certain risks which are obviously involved, I must ask the people to resist the slavery..."

Mahatma Gandhi, in the *Harijan*, 1942

"DO OR DIE"

The Quit India Resolution was passed by Congress on 7th August 1942. It approved "the launching of mass struggle on nonviolent lines on widest possible scale under the leadership of Gandhi". The AICC meeting went on late into the night on 8th August 1942, to flesh out the details.

As per instructions given by the Congress Committee, people were free to carry out the nonviolent campaign individually, in case their leader was absent. The movement captured the pulse of the people who were ready to give it their all.

> "Every one of you should, from this moment onwards, consider yourself a free man or woman and act as if you are free... We shall do or die..."
> Gandhi addressing a procession of Indians, 1942

True to their word of not tolerating any form of rebellion, the British government acted swiftly and put all leaders, right from Gandhi to Taluka Congress presidents, behind bars, before the dawn of 9th August 1942.

However, the movement was now beyond the control of the British. If the government thought that removal of leaders would dampen the spirit of the people, they were mistaken. On hearing the news of arrest of their leaders, people came out in thousands to protest.

Just before dawn, a police sergeant handed an arrest warrant to Asaf Ali. His wife and activist Aruna Asaf Ali accompanied him to the railway station, where she accidentally met Maulana Azad, who was supposed to address a mass gathering at Gowalia Tank Maidan in Bombay.

On an impulse, Aruna Asaf Ali made up her mind to stand in for Maulana Azad. However, the meeting was declared illegal and the police forced people to vacate the ground within two minutes. Without wasting a single minute, Aruna scrambled onto the stage. In a flurry,

Aruna Asaf Ali

she unfurled the Indian flag and screamed authoritatively, "Britishers, QUIT INDIA!"

She was arrested on the spot. Complete hartals were observed in various parts of India and peaceful processions were taken out across the country.

The British reacted to the slogan of 'Quit India' not only with lathi-charge but also bullets and pellets.

The police did not hesitate to fire mercilessly at point blank range at a 73-year-old woman named Matangini Hazra in Bengal. She succumbed to the bullet injury but her grip on the tricolour did not ease. The police did not even spare teenage schoolboys who were taking out a procession, carrying the tricolour. They shot sixteen-year-old Sirish Kumar, who was seen waving the Indian flag. He passed on the flag to the next boy who was shot dead too. It was passed on fifteen times until all the schoolboys had laid down their lives. Similarly, the police opened fire on a procession of students who were trying to hoist the flag at the Secretariat building in Patna. By the time the firing stopped, there were 7 dead, and 14 wounded. In their deaths, these young men showed the ruler what Gandhi meant when he raised the war cry of "Do or Die".

Their martyrdom was the pivotal event of 1942 which resulted in a mass eruption of protests in Bihar.

The nonviolent struggle for freedom was truly a battle of the people. Students joined the struggle in huge numbers and professionals left their jobs to participate and follow the war cry: Do or Die! Indira Gandhi, who had recently got married to Feroze Gandhi, also joined the struggle.

UNDERGROUND ACTIVITIES

Within the Congress, young socialists like Achyut Patwardhan, Rammanohar Lohia, Aruna Asaf Ali, N.G. Gore and S.M. Joshi became complete revolutionaries, under the leadership of Jayaprakash Narayan. They established secret organizations in all parts of India to carry on the "People's Revolution". Their aim was to paralyze the administration by disrupting communication channels. Their chief targets were post offices, telegraph wires, and the railways. The protesters also disrupted government establishments, especially police stations and the collectorates. In some instances, the revolutionary groups looted treasuries. In small towns and mofussils, the sheer number of protesters forced the administration to give up, with people establishing self-governments.

However, these violent activities could not last long as the British government crushed them with their superior force. One by one, revolutionaries were arrested and tortured in jail. However, peaceful resistance by the masses kept the struggle going, in spite of the fact that most of the leaders were jailed and there was no organizational leadership to steer the movement.

Right from Kashmir to Kanyakumari, and Kutch to Kamrup, young militant soldiers were fighting for freedom. Many such as the

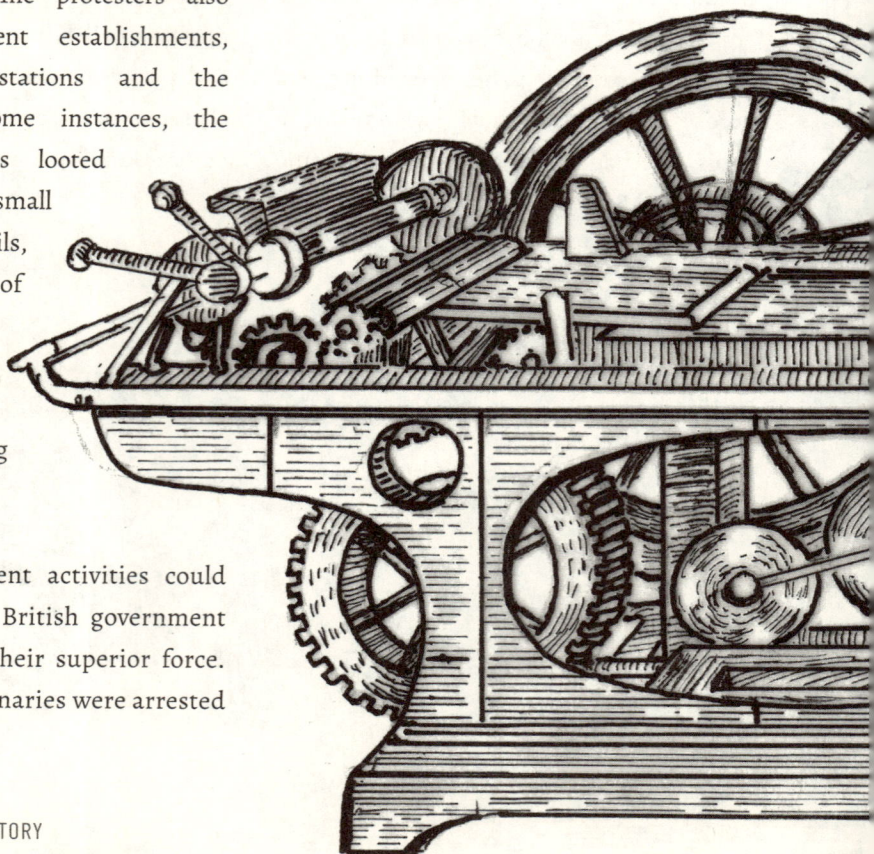

Azad Hind Fauj established their own radio stations, on which they broadcast news of their achievements. In Allahabad, young Indira Gandhi was looking after one such radio station. Many freedom activists also managed underground printing presses to bring out newspapers, journals and pamphlets in secret. Through these novel ways, people kept the Quit India struggle going for another three years.

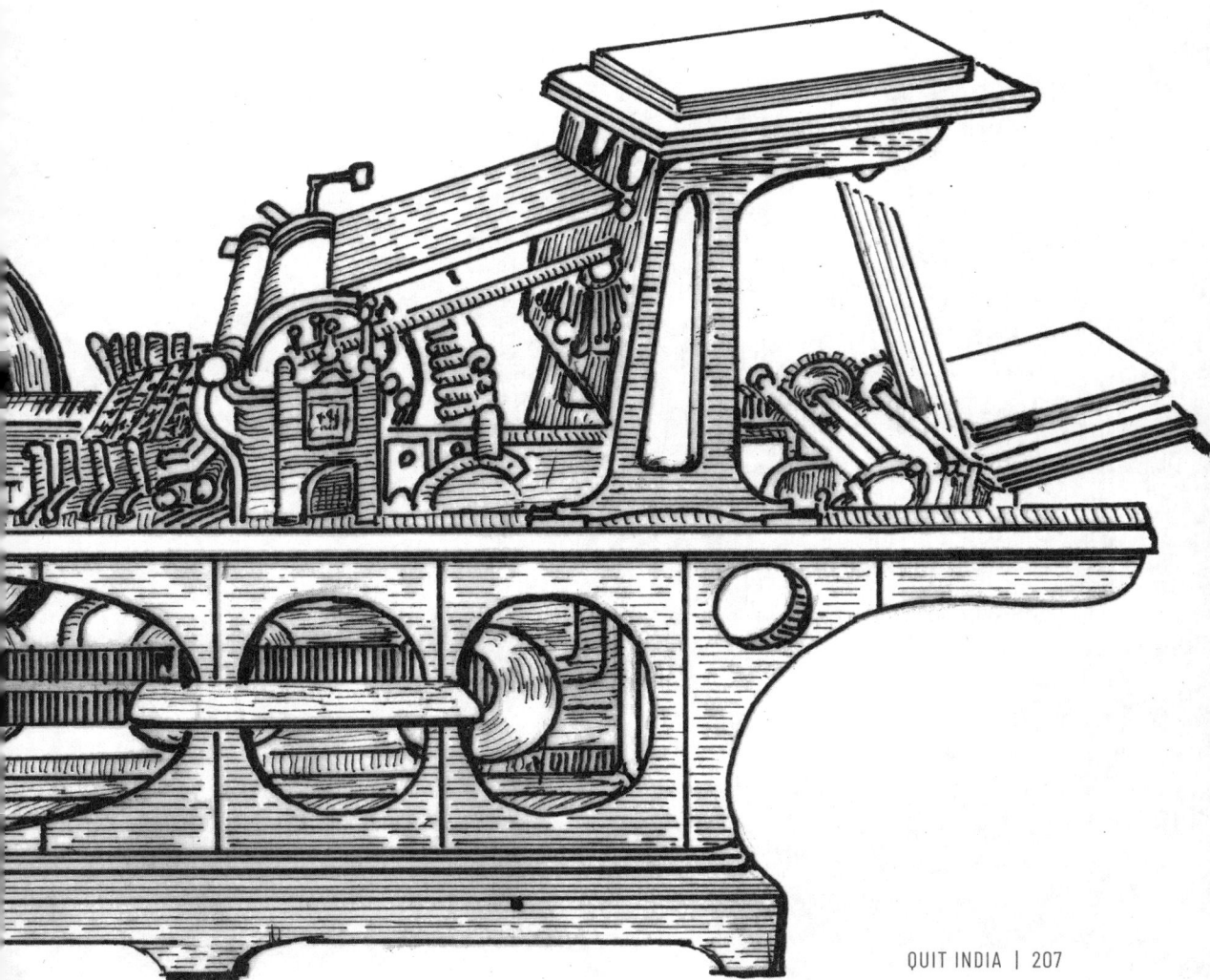

The British promised to leave India by July 1948, but Viceroy Mountbatten moved this forward to August 1947 due to communal tension.

FREEDOM
AT LAST!

1943 Gandhi Begins Fast • **1945** Labour Party Wins in Britain
• **1945** INA Trials Begin • **1946** Naval Revolt • **1946** Cabinet Mission
• **1947** Mountbatten Plan

The whole nation responded enthusiastically to the call of "Quit India", given by the Congress. But certain political parties remained uninvolved. The Muslim League asked Muslims to stay "completely aloof from the movement". The League also appealed to other countries to validate the Muslim demand for a separate state. Voicing the sentiment of many, Vinayak Damodar Savarkar of the Hindu Mahasabha declared the demand for Pakistan as "outrageous and treacherous".

Viceroy Linlithgow was in favour of a united India. His successor Lord Wavell had the same view. Incensed at these views, the Muslim League coined a new slogan "Divide and Quit".

As soon as Germany attacked Russia, the Communist Party of India changed its attitude and sided with Britain. The party helped the British government during the Quit India Movement. Many of its members acted as stooges and spies against their fellow countrymen.

Incidents of violence during the movement were upsetting to Gandhi.

> "If then I cannot get soothing balm for my pain, I must resort to the law prescribed for Satyagrahis, namely a fast according to capacity."
>
> Mahatma Gandhi on violence by the British

He went on a twenty-one day fast from 9th February to 2nd March 1943. The British government offered to release him during the fast, but Gandhi refused. The entire nation was tense. Leaders appealed to the Viceroy and the Prime Minister of Britain. There were loud protests. Three members of the Governor-General's Executive Council furnished resignations. But the government did not relent. The nation heaved a sigh of relief when Gandhi survived the fast.

Lord Linlithgow retired on 20th October 1943 and was succeeded by Lord Wavell. The country was in the grip of war-time shortages, which included essential commodities. India's resources were drained out to fight its colonizer's war. Prices were soaring high. More than fifty lakh people died in the Bengal famine.

Meanwhile, Gandhi faced personal tragedies when his wife Kasturba and close colleague Mahadev Desai died in the Agha Khan Palace, where both had been kept under house arrest. The nation paid an emotional homage to its Ba (mother) on 22nd February 1944. After the death of Kasturba, Gandhi's health started failing rapidly. Fearing that Gandhi might also lose his life, the British government released him to avoid further tragedy.

The First World War was not yet over, but the Allied forces had averted defeat and victory was in sight. The members of the Central Legislature held a general meeting, where along with members of the League, the legislature decided against a finance bill and other government measures.

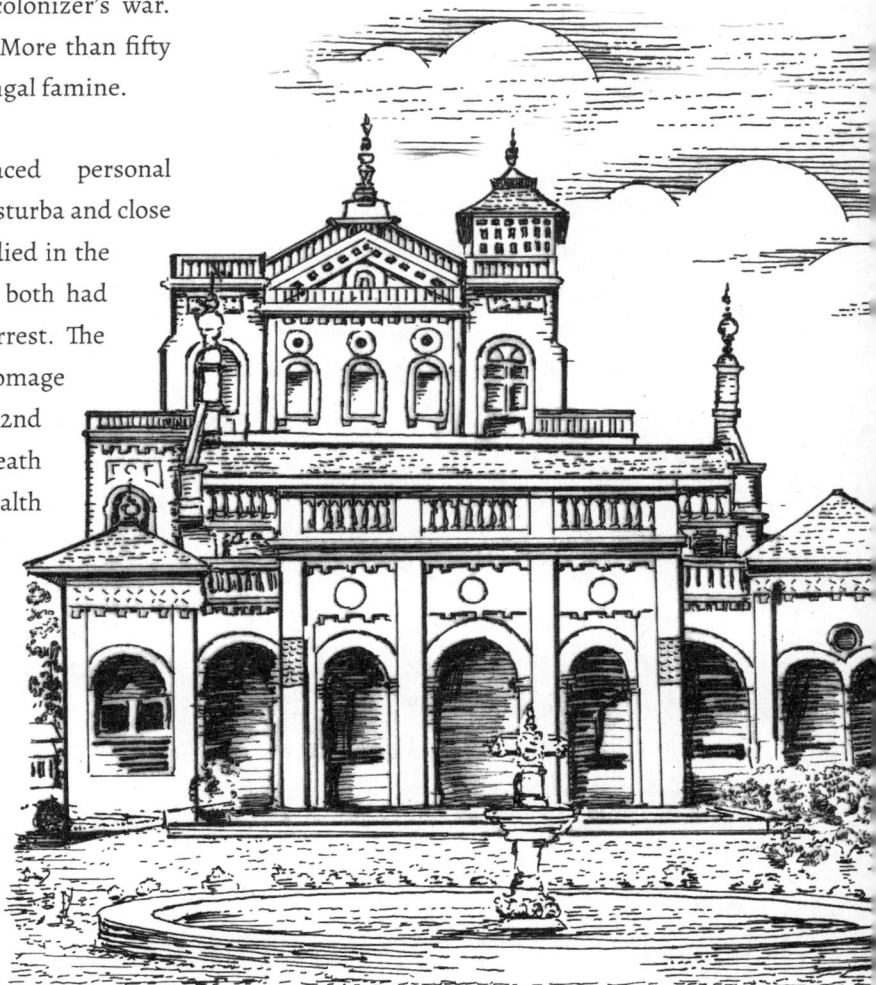

Aga Khan palace

FAILED NEGOTIATIONS

Gandhi tried to have an open discussion with the Viceroy but did not succeed. He proposed that the Congress and Muslim League should jointly take up the issue with the British government. Since 1942, C. Rajagopalachari, a sharp Congressman from Madras, had been preparing the ground for negotiations between the two parties. Even though Jinnah did not approve of Rajagopalachari's ideas, he agreed to meet Gandhi to discuss a possible solution.

Gandhi's offer of negotiating with the Muslim League irked the Hindus of Punjab and Bengal, as well as the Sikh minority of India. The talks went on for eighteen days from 9th to 27th September 1944. But no agreement was reached. Gandhi could not accept the contention that Muslims would form a separate state in India with the right of self-determination.

When the talks failed, the Viceroy was convinced that there could be no political agreement between the Congress and Muslim League. He took the initiative to form a transitional government at the Centre with representatives of all political parties. Before his departure to England to seek necessary approvals, prominent freedom fighter and lawyer Sir Tej Bahadur Sapru tried to frame a Constitution acceptable to both the Congress and the Muslim League. However, Jinnah and Dr. Ambedkar refused to cooperate with Sapru.

Bhulabhai Desai, a Congressmen, who also attempted to bring about an agreement on the Constitution, was more successful. Muslim League's Liaquat Ali Khan agreed to Desai's plan to form an Interim Government at the Centre with equal number of Hindus and Muslims in the Executive Council. Only the Governor-General and Commander-in-Chief were to be non-Indians. Though Desai claimed that both Gandhi and Jinnah had agreed to this plan, Jinnah shocked the nation by denying any knowledge of the plan. Despite Gandhi's approval to the plan, other Congress leaders did not agree. Desai stepped back in utter disappointment, just like Rajagopalachari.

Lord Wavell soon left for London.

SIMLA CONFERENCE

After discussing the plan for an Interim Government with the Cabinet, Lord Wavell returned to India and immediately called a conference in Simla, inviting twenty-one leaders representing all political parties. On 25th June 1945, the leaders were to discuss the composition of the new Executive Council of the Governor-General. Except the Governor-General and Commander-in-Chief, all other members were to be Indians. Equal number of positions were to be given to caste Hindus and Muslims. A British High Commissioner was to be appointed in India to look after commercial and other interests of Britain. The new Executive Council was also prepared to fight the war against Japan and was to govern on behalf of the British government until a permanent Constitution could be agreed upon. It would also work out how such an agreement could be brought about.

The press and public welcomed the plan. Gandhi did not approve the classification "Caste Hindu", which the Congress was to represent. Jinnah insisted that Muslim members of the council must be from the Muslim League. The Hindu Mahasabha felt neglected as it was not included in the Conference and was also not in favour of equal representation of Hindus and Muslims in the Council.

All Congress Working Committee members, who had been jailed by the British, were released on 14th June 1945, for the purpose of attending the Conference. The invited leaders met five times. Each time, Jinnah insisted that Muslim members of the Executive Council must be chosen from among members of the Muslim League. Members from the Scheduled Caste wanted representation on the same principle as in the case of Muslims. Their representative N. Sivaraj challenged the Congress claim to nominate Scheduled Caste representatives. Jinnah also demanded additional safeguards against the Viceroy's veto to protect Muslim interests. However, Lord Wavell did not give in to all the demands made by Jinnah and the Conference was dissolved without any success. The failure of the Conference was a success for the Muslim League, which now emerged as the decisive factor to make or mar the future settlement.

Mohammad Ali Jinnah

TRANSFER OF POWER

On 26th July 1945, the Labour Party came into power in Britain after winning the general election. Britain had lost its supremacy in world politics after the Second World War. The country had suffered tremendous loss of manpower, money and materials. America and Russia emerged as the new world powers.

The emergence of Bose's Indian National Army and its role during the war made the British realize that the loyalty of their soldiers could not be taken for granted. However, it managed to stop the military advances of the INA through superior military strength. On the

INA soldiers carrying the Azad Hind flag

Similarly, representatives of princely states would also be asked to suggest ways for their participation in the Constitution-making body. Till the Constitution was framed, an Executive Council having the support of all political parties would be established to carry on the government.

The Congress Working Committee met in September 1945, in Bombay. It reiterated its belief in a united India, without forcing anyone to remain a part of it against his or her will. Since the Congress failed to reach an understanding with the Muslim League, it decided to approach the Muslim masses directly to win them over.

other hand, the moral force of the nonviolent resistance was difficult to counter.

Lord Wavell again left for London to hold talks with His Majesty's government on 24th August 1945. On 18th September, in his national broadcast, Wavell announced that the Constituent Assembly would be called upon to discuss whether the proposals of the 1942 Declaration were acceptable to them, or some other alternative needed to be worked out.

Ahead of the general elections for legislatures, the majority of Muslims chose the Muslim League. But the nationalist Muslims remained with the Congress. This made the two parties the key players in the forthcoming elections. The Congress was not at its best due to the absence of its leaders, who were put in jails by the British. However, it prepared itself to fight these elections with all its might.

THE INFAMOUS INA TRIAL

Just then, the infamous INA trial sent shock waves through the country. The Indian National Army formed by Bose had many Indian soldiers who had deserted the British Indian Army. After the surrender of Japan, these 25,000 soldiers were put on trial and a military tribunal was set up for this purpose. In the first batch, three officers Shah Nawaz Khan (Muslim), Prem Kumar Sehgal (Hindu), and Gurbaksh Singh Dhillon (Sikh) were put on public trial at the historic Red Fort. For the public, they were heroes who had fought with valour for the freedom of their country. The Congress leaders chose to defend the soldiers under trial. Bhulabhai Desai, Sir Tej Bahadur and Jawaharlal Nehru donned the lawyer's gown to fight their case.

The trial evoked nationwide excitement. The Muslim League too associated itself with the trial. Protests and demonstrations were held against the prosecution throughout India. The three INA members were found guilty. They were, however, not given the death sentence but dismissed from service and handed transportation for life, which too was remitted. The three were then released and welcomed as heroes.

In the provincial elections, Congress emerged a clear winner, securing fifty-seven seats. The Muslim League got thirty and the rest of the seats went to the Hindu Mahasabha, Akali Sikhs and Independents. Even in some Muslim-majority states, the Muslim League did not get an absolute majority. Meanwhile, Jinnah conceded to a parliamentary delegation from England that he would not like non-Muslim areas of Punjab to be included in Pakistan. He wanted Pakistan to remain within the British Empire with a British Governor-General. Jawaharlal Nehru emphasized that if at all Pakistan had to be conceded, it should be done after taking the opinion of people residing in the border districts.

The Viceroy declared that a new Executive Council would be formed by political leaders and a Constitution-making body would be established as soon as possible. But before these two bodies could be formed, the Indian Naval Revolt of 1946 rocked the country.

NAVAL REVOLT

A group of Indians serving in the Royal Indian Navy, who were posted at the Signal School in Bombay, went on a hunger strike, as a mark of protest against low pay and racial discrimination. The trigger was their British commander's derogatory remarks about Indians. The revolt was strengthened when Indians serving in other establishments of the navy also joined them.

The situation got out of control when these protesting naval workers captured some ships and threatened to open fire on military guards. Thanks to the efforts of Sardar Vallabhbhai Patel, the ugly situation and resultant tragedy was averted when the naval ratings surrendered on 23rd February 1946. However, rebellion was still being expressed through strikes and protests. Similar discontentment was also simmering in the army and the air force, though it did not surface the way it did in the navy.

CABINET MISSION

Judging by the deteriorating situation, the British government, under Attlee, decided to expedite the Constitutional process and sent a special mission consisting of three Cabinet Ministers: Lord Pethick Lawrence, Sir Stafford Cripps and A.V. Alexander.

The Cabinet Mission arrived in Delhi on 24th March 1946. Congress President Maulana Azad represented the party and proposed that the Constitution-making body should determine the nature of the Constitution. The Congress also proposed that the Interim Government at the Centre should be responsible for all matters, including setting up of the Constitution-making body. As the elections had already taken place, eleven provincial representatives should be selected after ascertaining the preference of provincial governments. The other four members of the Interim Government should be representatives of minorities. As for the Constitution, the Congress preferred federal government with minimum compulsory federal subjects like defence, communications and foreign affairs. The rest would come under the jurisdiction of the provincial government.

Thus, provinces were left with three choices:

1 To stand out of the Constitution.

2 To join the Constitution, allowing compulsory subjects of defence, foreign affairs, communication and finance to be dealt with by the Centre.

3 To surrender all the subjects to the Centre.

The Cabinet Mission also suggested that few more seats could be given to Muslims in case they got lesser seats due to the above formula.

Meanwhile, Gandhi rejected the Two-Nation Theory of Jinnah and also objected to two Constitution-making bodies. He suggested that first Jinnah should be approached to form the government from the elected members of the legislature. The Congress should be given the chance to form the government only if Jinnah refused.

Jinnah argued for the case of Pakistan and maintained that Hindus and Muslims differed socially and culturally and could never live in harmony as one nation. Therefore, there was no other way but to divide India. At the same time, he carefully avoided the question of Pakistan's administrative feasibility, given the geographical unity of India. The statistics collected by the Cabinet Mission showed that even in the Muslim-dominated provinces, out of which Jinnah wanted to carve out Pakistan, the Hindus amounted to 41.31 percent of the total population – a considerably large minority.

Sikhs and the Scheduled Castes were also divided over the matter. The two groups could not represent their views unanimously except for the demand of special provision to safeguard their rights and interests.

Jinnah took an aggressive posture. He threatened that any attempt to force the Constitution and Interim Government not acceptable to the Muslim League would be resisted by all possible means by the Muslims of India. In spite of this threat, the Cabinet Mission put forth the logic that establishment of Pakistan, whether large or small, would not solve the communal problem. The mission also enumerated the administrative, military and economic difficulties the two nations would have to face if the country was divided. They pointed out the distance and resultant difficulty in communication between two halves of the proposed Pakistan.

"Let me tell you that Muslim India will not rest content until we have established full, complete, sovereign Pakistan..."

Jinnah to the Muslim League, on the Cabinet Mission Plan, 1946

After arguing about the non-feasibility of two nations, the Cabinet Mission recommended:

1 Union of India consisting of British-ruled India and princely states. The union should deal with foreign affairs, defence and communications. The union could tax to earn finances required for these departments.

2 The Union should have an Executive and Legislature with representatives of British India and princely states. Any communal issue would be decided by the majority from each community, as well as majority of representatives who were present and voting.

3 All other subjects were left to provinces and states.

4 Provinces and states were free to form groups, with one Executive and Legislature, and decide upon common subjects.

5 Lastly, the constitutions of union and group could reconsider the term of their constitutions after every ten years.

The Constitution-making body was to be formed from the representatives of the provinces elected on the basis of population. The two communities would get seats according to their population in each province. The provincial representatives were to be selected by the elected members of that community in the Legislative Assembly, as in the case of the present Rajya Sabha.

There were many differences over the composition of the proposed Interim Government. When the two major parties, the Congress and the Muslim League, could not reach a consensus, the Viceroy proposed the names of fourteen members, six from the Congress, including one from a Scheduled Caste, five from the Muslim League, and one representative each from the Sikh, Christian and Parsi communities. By implication, it meant that Jinnah's proposal was accepted. The Congress refused to be part of the Interim Government but decided to join the proposed Constituent Assembly.

DIRECT ACTION

The All-India Congress Committee met on 6th and 7th July 1946 and accepted the Cabinet Mission Plan. Jawaharlal Nehru replaced Maulana Azad as the President of the Congress, and made it clear that the Congress had agreed to form a Constituent Assembly, which was empowered to frame the Constitution of its choice.

The Muslim League agreed to the Cabinet Mission Plan as it thought that having a weak Centre and provinces with considerable powers would safeguard the Muslims. But he soon withdrew his support on issues such as grouping and composition of the Interim Government. He gave the call of "Direct Action" at the Working Committee meeting of the Muslim League. On 16th August 1946, also known as Direct Action Day, unprecedented riots and violence broke out throughout the country.

Calcutta suffered the worst fate. Thousands were killed and many injured in the communal clashes. The Muslim League Ministry, under H.S. Suhrawardy, played it cool and resisted taking immediate action. The havoc created in Calcutta made the government realize that unless some understanding was brought about immediately, the Calcutta horror could be repeated all over the country. Therefore, the British government decided to go ahead with the nominations for the Interim Government. The firm attitude of the government made Jinnah relent. The Muslim League agreed to join the government on 13th October 1946 and sent the names of its five nominees.

Maulana Azad

INTERIM GOVERNMENT

With the Congress and the Muslim League on board, the Interim Government started functioning. But communal bickering was creating violent situations. Gandhi, true to his faith in nonviolence, first toured Noakhali to appease the Muslims and then went to Bihar to spread the message of love among the Hindus. The Muslim League under Jinnah tried to delay the summoning of the Constituent Assembly. However, the British government stood firm and declared that the Constituent Assembly be held on 9th December 1946.

Not a single Muslim League member attended the assembly. The League renounced the composition and procedure of the Constituent Assembly as "illegal and invalid". As a result, the Congress and other minorities demanded the resignation of the Muslim League members from the Interim Government. However, the Muslim League was not ready to resign. While the Viceroy expressed his sympathy towards the party, the Congress threatened to withdraw from the Interim Government. The situation became really tense. Any moment, communal riots leading to a civil war could have erupted.

Realizing the gravity of the situation, British Prime Minister Clement Attlee, despite opposition from Viceroy Wavell, declared, on 20th February 1946, at the House of Commons that the British would quit India. He announced the deadline of June 1948 for the transfer of power to the Indians.

This firm declaration increased political activity in India. The Muslim League tried

to consolidate its position in the provinces it wished to include in Pakistan. In Assam, they resorted to direct action, instigating violence, but the response was poor. In the North-West Frontier Province, Congress lost ground to the Muslim League. The Muslim League was successful in establishing its ministry in Sindh.

In Punjab, the situation turned violent when Akali Sikhs and Hindus resisted the formation of a Muslim League government. The communal riots forced the Governor to take over the administration. The Congress realized the futility of insisting on the unity of India and agreed to the partition of Punjab, accepting the British interpretation of the Cabinet Mission Plan. They asked the Muslim League to discuss the method of transfer of power. The Communist Party also supported the demand for Pakistan "as a just programme and rational".

THE INEVITABLE

The appointment of Lord Mountbatten as Governor-General of India on 24th March 1947 proved to be a definite step to expedite the transfer of power to Indians. Lord Mountbatten was a practical man, who wasted no time in starting a dialogue with Indian leaders. After discussing the issue with Jinnah, Mountbatten declared that Jinnah was "hell bent on Pakistan". His visit to NWFP and Punjab, where he could see the results of communal frenzy, convinced him that settlement should be expedited and that the partition of India was inevitable.

It caused great mental agony to Congress leaders to give up the ideal of Indian unity, but it seemed that the only way to avoid further massacre of innocent people in communal frenzy was to accept the idea of Partition. One by one, the Congress leaders reconciled themselves to the two-nation theory. The first to accept the Partition was Sardar Vallabhbhai Patel.

"Whether we liked it or not, there were two nations in India."

Sardar Patel, as quoted by Abul Kalam Azad in *India Wins Freedom*, 1958

Nehru, who had completely rejected the idea of Partition at first, came round to it in order to avoid further delay and mass killing. On behalf of the Congress, Nehru conveyed to the Viceroy that Congress would accept Partition provided Punjab and Bengal were divided.

Gandhi declared vehemently that Partition would take place "over my dead body".

Though Gandhi could never fully agree to the two-nation theory, he reconciled to the decision, announcing at a prayer meeting:

"If both of us – Hindus and Muslims - cannot agree on anything else, the Viceroy is left with no choice."

THE MOUNTBATTEN PLAN

Lord Mountbatten

Things moved fast from this point onwards. After getting the leaders to agree on the Partition, Mountbatten left for London on 2nd May 1947, to submit the plan for the division of India to His Majesty's government. He received the approval of the Cabinet with certain modifications. The approved plan divided India not only in two but into many autonomous states. It gave the provinces a choice to either join one of the two nations, Pakistan and India, or to remain as independent states.

Statesman Huseyn Shaheed Suhrawardy and Sarat Chandra Bose came up with the idea of giving the choice to provinces to remain as independent sovereign states. The proposal was accepted by the British, but when Lord Mountbatten showed it to Nehru, he rejected it vehemently. Things would have come to a standstill, but for a new plan suggested by V.P. Menon, an Indian official in the Viceroy's Secretariat. Menon suggested that Punjab and Bengal be divided, and predominantly non-Muslim parts of Punjab and Bengal should remain in India and the Muslim-majority areas should join Pakistan. After consulting the Congress, the Muslim League and the

Sikhs, Mountbatten submitted the plan to the Cabinet. The plan in its final form was as follows:

In Punjab and Bengal, Hindu and Muslim members of the Provincial Legislative Assembly representing two dominant communities were to meet separately and vote in favour or against the partition of provinces. If a simple majority on both sides decided on Partition, the province would be divided. The Sindh Provincial Legislature was to decide whether the Constitution should be framed by them or a new body should be elected. The elected members of the NWF Province were to be given the opportunity to reconsider their position. They would have to decide whether to frame the Constitution along with the members of the part of Punjab which would join

Pakistan, or elect a new body. Similarly, British Baluchistan was to be given the opportunity to reconsider its fate.

In Assam, except for Sylhet district, Hindus formed the majority. In case Bengal was partitioned, the Sylhet population would have to decide whether to remain in Assam or join the new East Bengal Province of Pakistan.

The Boundary Commission set up by the Governor-General was to demarcate the boundary lines. Lord Mountbatten announced the above approved plan to Indians on 3rd June 1947 and declared that transfer of power might take place as early as 15th August 1947.

The Working Committee met in Delhi a day before the new plan was announced by Lord Mountbatten. Abdul Ghaffar Khan, known as Frontier Gandhi, was so distressed that he exclaimed, "Frontier would regard it as an act of treachery if the Congress now throw the Khudai Khidmatgars to the wolves". Gandhi and Khan appealed to Lord Mountbatten for reconsideration. But Mountbatten would not make any exceptions.

The Congress Working Committee in its Delhi session on 14th and 15th June 1947 passed the resolution to accept the partition of India.

The resolution was passed with 157 votes in its favour, 29 against and 32 neutral votes. The Council of the All-India Muslim League also accepted the Partition plan on 3rd June 1947.

As was expected, West Punjab and East Bengal, Sindh and NWFP opted for Pakistan, while East Punjab and West Bengal decided to join India. The district of Sylhet voted in favour of joining East Bengal, that is Pakistan.

On 4th July 1947, the Indian Independence Bill was introduced in the British Parliament and was passed without any amendment on 15th July 1947. The king put his seal of approval on the Bill on 18th July 1947.

Thus, according to the Indian Independence Act of 1947:

1. Two independent dominions, India and Pakistan, would be set up from 15th August 1947.

2. Pakistan would consist of Sindh, British Baluchistan, NWFP, West Punjab and East Bengal. The boundaries of Bengal and Punjab were to be determined by the Boundary Commission consisting of two members of Congress, and two of Muslim League, under the Chairmanship of Sir Cyril Radcliff. In case of disagreement, the chairman was to give his award.

3. A Governor-General for each dominion would be appointed by His Majesty.

4. The legislature of these two dominions would have full powers to make laws for their own dominion. No act of British Parliament would apply to these dominions from 15th August 1947.

5. From 15th August 1947, His Majesty's Government would not have any responsibility in governance of these two dominions and all treaties and agreements made by the British government with Indian princely states and tribals would lapse.

6. The Constituent Assembly of each dominion would become the Central Legislature to make laws for its own dominion.

Lord Mountbatten was appointed Governor-General of India, while Jinnah took over the post in Pakistan.

The controversy over the international status of these dominions was solved when the UNO recommended that membership of all international organizations, along with rights and obligations, would be given to India, and Pakistan was free to apply for membership of international organizations of her choice.

On 7th August 1947, Jinnah left for Karachi to see his dream come true. Lord Mountbatten also reached Karachi and addressed the Constituent Assembly. Jinnah was appointed Governor-General of Pakistan.

Amidst all this, one lonely man, who had aroused the masses to fight a unique nonviolent battle against the mightiest power in the world, was busy applying the balm of love on the victims of communal frenzy. Gandhi was touring the provinces of riot-stricken Noakhali and the surrounding areas to console his distraught countrymen.

On 14th August 1947, as thousands of diyas illuminated the dark monsoon night, the light of hope entered the lives of Indians. All roads leading to the Parliament House were packed with people. Men and women could be seen dancing with joy, chanting the slogans "Bharat Mata ki Jai" and "Gandhiji ki Jai".

Inside the Parliament, the mood was solemn. At the stroke of midnight, the traditional conch-shell was blown to announce the arrival of freedom. To the refrain of Vande Mataram, the song which had inspired thousands to give up their lives for the sake of their motherland, the Union Jack was lowered. The Indian tricolour flew triumphantly against the midnight sky.

Once again, the spirit of man had triumphed. This victory was unique because it had been achieved by the use of a new weapon – the weapon of nonviolence. Till now, victories were won by firing bullets, cannons and bombs. But these violent methods always begot violence.

The dream of a nation had come true.

"We want deeper sincerity of motive, a greater courage in speech and earnestness in action."

Sarojini Naidu

"From tomorrow, we shall be delivered from the bondage of the British rule. But from midnight today, India will be partitioned too. While, therefore, tomorrow will be a day of rejoicing, it will be a day of sorrow as well. It will throw a heavy burden of responsibility upon us. Let us pray to God that He may give us strength to bear it."

Mohandas Karamchand Gandhi

"In attaining our ideals, our means should be as pure as the end."

Dr. Rajendra Prasad

"Independence is no doubt a matter of joy. But let us not forget that this independence has thrown on us greater responsibilities. By independence, we have lost the excuse of blaming the British for anything going wrong. If hereafter things go wrong, we will have nobody to blame except ourselves. There is a greater danger of things going wrong. Times are fast-changing."

Dr. Bhimrao Ramji Ambedkar

"At the stroke of the midnight hour, when the world sleeps, India will awake to life and freedom. A moment comes, which comes but rarely in history, when we step out from the old to the new – when an age ends, and when the soul of a nation, long suppressed, finds utterance."

Jawaharlal Nehru, on the eve of India's independence

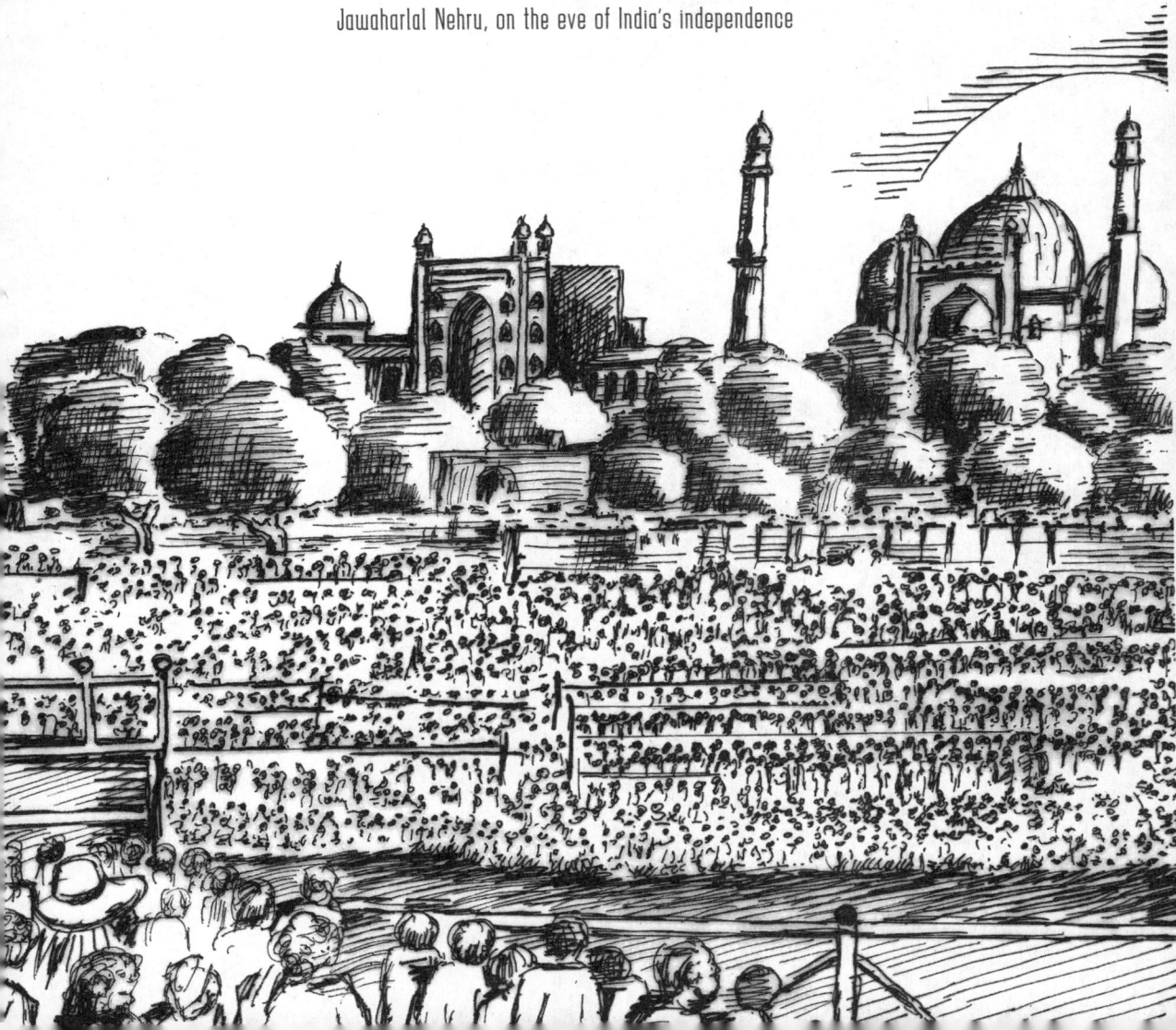

India owes her Constitution to
Dr. Bhimrao Ramji Ambedkar, a multi-
faceted man who remapped the frontiers of
human achievement through sheer tenacity.

THE CONSTITUTION OF INDIA

1946 First Meeting of the Constituent Assembly • **1949** Constitution Day • **1966** Tashkent Declaration • **1984** Death of Indira Gandhi

On 9th December 1946, the Constituent Assembly, consisting of elected members from all provinces and princely states, met for the first time and devoted itself to the task of drafting the Constitution of India, under the Chairmanship of Dr. Rajendra Prasad. The time had come to fulfil the pledge taken against the Simon Commission in 1928, and in the true spirit of nation building, create the fundamentals of governance, before the transfer of power by the British to India.

The Constituent Assembly, comprising elected and nominated members, eminent scholars and lawyers representing all states, princely states, religions and various sections of society, set itself the marathon task of drafting the Constitution of India. The Assembly had 389 members – 296 from British Indian provinces, 93 from princely states and 15 others. The Congress won 208 seats, while the Muslim League got 73 seats. Pursuing his claim for a separate Muslim nation of Pakistan, Jinnah withdrew from the Constituent Assembly.

The Constitution of India is the modern sacred text of contemporary India. It reflects the new aspirations and values of the people of India and testifies how Indians are the supreme masters in all matters concerning their welfare. Through lengthy discussions and debates on every proposal, the Acts and Articles of the Constitution were framed, based on the essential tenets of democracy, republicanism, civil liberties, and economic and social justice. Indians were framing their own Constitution, which was not a mere emulation of the British Parliament but a structure resting on democratic ideals. It had to reflect the spirit of the struggle for Independence, setting the guidelines and principles of an emerging nation.

The Indian Constitution begins with "We, the People of India..." the most beautiful phrase in the Preamble of the Constitution, signifying the voice of people who were under subjugation for years, finally holding their head high in front of the whole world, embodying the spirit of the Constitution.

The Preamble encapsulates the fundamental structure of the Constitution, stressing on Justice, Liberty and Equality by a democratic form of government of a Republic in which the people hold supreme. Having been framed by the "people of India", the Constitution does not allow for any sort of discrimination on the basis of religion or race, and therefore, secularism is implied in all its guidelines. It ensures the citizens' entitlement of rights, pertaining to Equality, Education, Freedom, Religion and Right against Exploitation. The Indian Constitution establishes sovereignty, a socialist republic and a democratic state. It functions as an equal representative body to all sections of society and provides a secular environment for all citizens of the country.

SALIENT FEATURES OF THE CONSTITUTION

- As a sovereign country, its people possess the power to elect their own representatives for the Parliament.

- As a socialist nation, there will be no discrimination on the basis of race, sex, colour, language and creed.

- As a republic nation, the President of the country will function democratically through the preference of people.

- As a democracy, every citizen of the country is entitled to his or her right to function as a responsible person of the country.

- As written law, the Constitution lays out a set of instructions to regulate the functioning of its various organs such as the judiciary, the Parliament and other structures within the Constitution.

- As a foundation of a country, the Constitution represents the people of the country and what effectively belongs to each one of them.

The Indian Constitution consists of 395 Articles, divided into 22 parts with 12 schedules and 94 constitutional amendments. The document is a constitution for both the Centre and the States of the Indian Union. It is the longest constitution ever drafted in the history of mankind, much bigger than the US Constitution and the French Constitution, with 7 Articles and 89 Articles respectively.

The herculean task of writing the Constitution of India was taken up by several men and women from diverse political thought. These included nationalists, Gandhians, eminent lawyers and knowledgeable thinkers. To tackle a wide spectrum of subjects, different committees and sub-committees were formed to prepare a basic draft for debates to be approved and passed on to the drafting committee. The six most active and influential members were Jawaharlal Nehru, Vallabhbhai Patel, B.R. Ambedkar, Maulana Azad, Sarojini Naidu and Rajendra Prasad. They ironed out the teething troubles, which included proper rehabilitation of refugees from Pakistan, food shortages, law and order issues, and communal riots flaring up in many parts of the country.

The Constituent Assembly had fifteen women from different regions of the country who belonged to diverse social backgrounds. They were: Ammu Swaminathan, Begum Aizaz Rasul, Dakshayani Velayudhan, Durgabai Deshmukh, Purnima Banerjee, Sucheta Kripalani, Kamala Chaudhary, Leela Roy, Hansa Jivraj Mehta, Renuka Ray, Malati Choudhury, Rajkumari Amrit Kaur, Vijaya Lakshmi Pandit, Annie Mascarene and Sarojini Naidu. All these illustrious individuals had worked on women's emancipation and equal rights, with each having an inspiring story to tell. Most had exemplary careers in areas of social work, politics, literature and nation building.

B.R. AMBEDKAR

B.R. Ambedkar is often called the architect of the Indian Constitution, credited with giving a final shape to the massive document. The most qualified person for the role of Chairman of the Drafting Committee, Ambedkar was known for his great scholarship in jurisprudence and constitutional laws. He was a great spokesperson not just for the rights of Dalits and Harijans but also women. As a Law Minister, Ambedkar introduced reservations for Dalits in education and government jobs.

Born on 14th April 1891, to Dalit parents who were then considered "untouchable" by the caste-ridden Hindu society, Bhimrao Ramji Ambedkar had suffered discrimination right from his childhood. At school, he had to sit outside on a gunny bag to attend classes and was never allowed to play with or share food with classmates. He was barred from drinking water from the common well. Ambedkar didn't let caste-based humiliation come in the way of achieving great things. He earned four doctorates from prominent institutions such as Columbia University and the London School of Economics, and also earned a law degree from Gray's Inn, one of the four Inns of Court in London, to become a barrister. A knowledgeable jurist and compassionate social reformist, Ambedkar stressed upon equality and legal rights for all classes in the Constitution.

The Constitution of India clearly establishes three main structures of the government – the Judiciary, the Legislature and the Executive.

Thus, the Constitution outlines the functions of all these three structures for the benefit of the citizens of the country. Made with democratic ideals and a vision of autonomy, the Indian Constitution is the first and last word in Indian law and governance, and lays down the national goals of democracy, socialism, secularism and national integration, outlining the rights, duties and obligations of the Indian Citizen.

THE FUNDAMENTAL RIGHTS

Primarily, the Indian Constitution is a social document. British and other western thinkers assumed that a poor country with an illiterate majority would not be able to devise the principles of rules and rights of people, forgetting that these masses had been preparing for this moment for decades during the freedom struggle.

Indians had a first-hand experience of witnessing the unfair practices of the British rulers, which were based on exploitation and segregation. People had endured unfair punishment and extortion without any recourse to justice. Aware of the needs of every citizen, the Constitution makers ensured that the Fundamental Rights and Directive Principles rest upon the notions of equality and equal opportunity to all and are thus articulated in Part III and IV of the Constitution.

The Fundamental Rights give us the right to live with freedom as equal citizens. It includes freedom of speech that allows a free press and the right of all individuals to express their opinion without fear. The horrors of unequal caste system were made illegal, to ensure that all were treated as equal before the law. At the heart of democracy, the Fundamental Rights protect the citizens from a dictatorial government, and exploitation by the rich and powerful.

The Directive Principles are more like instructions from the Constitution to the government that enforce guidelines to the legislatures and executives of both the Indian states and the Central government. The six Fundamental Rights recognized by the Constitution are:

- **Right to Equality:** It provides for equality before law, end of discrimination, equality of opportunity, abolition of untouchability and abolition of titles.
- **Right to Freedom:** It incorporates six fundamental freedoms – freedom of speech and expression, freedom to form associations, freedom to assemble peaceably and without arms, freedom to move freely in India, freedom of residence in any part, and freedom to adopt any profession, trade or occupation. It ensures personal freedom and protection in respect of conviction for certain offences.
- **Right against exploitation:** This fundamental right prohibits sale and purchase of human beings, forced labour and employment of children in hazardous jobs and factories.
- **Right to Freedom of Religion:** It involves the freedom of conscience, religion and worship. Any person can follow the religion of their choice. It gives all religions freedom to establish and maintain their religious institutions.
- **Cultural and Educational Rights:** The Constitution guarantees the rights of the minorities to maintain and develop their languages and cultures. It also confers upon them the right to establish, maintain and administer their educational institutions.
- **Right to Constitutional Remedies:** It provides for the enforcement and protection of Fundamental Rights by the courts. It empowers the Supreme Court and High Courts to issue writs for the enforcement of these rights.

THE DIRECTIVE PRINCIPLES

This is the most striking feature of the Indian Constitution. The Directive Principles are instructions to the state for securing socio-economic developmental objectives through its policies. These are to be implemented by both the Union and the States. Directive Principles direct the state to ensure adequate means of livelihood, fairer distribution of wealth, equal pay for equal work, protection of children, women, labour and youth, old age pension, social security, local self-government, protection of the interests of the weaker sections of society, promotion of cottage industries, rural development, international peace and friendship and co-operation with other states etc. The Directive Principles centred on the duties of the State were inspired by Gandhi for the welfare of the people.

THE FUNDAMENTAL DUTIES

Just as the Constitution features the duties of the State towards its citizens, it also emphasizes duties of the citizens for their country.

- Respect for the Constitution, the national flag and the national anthem
- Cherish the noble ideals of the freedom struggle
- Uphold and protect the sovereignty, unity and integrity of India
- Defend the country and render national service when called upon to do so
- Advocate brotherhood among people and espouse dignity of women
- Preserve the rich heritage of the nation's composite culture
- Promote the natural environment and compassion for living creatures
- Develop scientific temper, humanism and spirit of inquiry
- Safeguard public property and abnegate violence
- Strive for excellence in all individual and collective activity
- Obligation of parents to provide opportunities for education to their children, as the case may be, ward between the age of six and fourteen years.

The Fundamental Duties are, however, not enforceable by the courts.

India is a single independent and sovereign state where all citizens enjoy common uniform citizenship. All men and women, above the age of 18 years, have an equal right to vote. Every registered voter gets the opportunity to vote in elections.

The Constitution provides for a Bicameral Legislature at the Union level, calling it the Union Parliament.

Bicameralism is the practice of having two Houses of Parliament.

Its two Houses are: the Lok Sabha and the Rajya Sabha. The Lok Sabha is the lower, popular, directly elected house of the Parliament, which represents the people of India. The Rajya Sabha is the upper and indirectly elected second House of the Parliament, which represents the states of the Indian Union. Of the two houses, the Lok Sabha is more powerful, with financial powers outlined clearly in the Constitution, alongside other procedures

and proceedings of the Parliament. However, the Rajya Sabha is neither as powerless as the British House of Lords nor is the Lok Sabha as powerful as the British House of Commons.

The Constitution of India provides for a parliamentary system of government at the Centre and the state level. The President of India is the constitutional head of state with nominal powers. The Union Council of Ministers headed by the Prime Minister is the real executive. Ministers are essentially the members of the Union Parliament. For all its policies and decisions, the Council of Ministers is collectively responsible to the Lok Sabha, which can remove the Ministry or Minister by passing a vote of no-confidence. The Cabinet, mainly the Prime Minister, has the power to get the Lok Sabha dissolved by the President. On similar lines, a parliamentary government is at work in each state.

The Judiciary, on the other hand, is independent of the political structure of the government. The Constitution provides for a single integrated judicial system for the Union and the states. The Supreme Court of

India works at the apex level, high courts at the state level and other courts work under the high courts.

However, the Constitution is the supreme law of the land, which incorporates the constitutional law of India. The Supreme Court acts as the guardian protector and interpreter of the Constitution. It is also the guardian of the Fundamental Rights of the people, whereby the Supreme Court determines the constitutional validity of all laws made by the legislatures. It can reject any law which is found to be unconstitutional. Through the Public Interest Litigation (PIL) system and by exerting its own powers, the Indian judiciary has been actively trying to secure public needs due to them, under the laws and policies of the state.

The articles and the structures of the Indian Constitution provide citizens with the rights and liberties. It is this written constitution that promises the citizens of the country their sovereignty, describes the fundamental rights, directive principles and fundamental duties of the inhabitants. It follows a rigid as well as flexible system that is centrally governed by the government of the country, allowing for amendments and additions to the original draft of the Constitution, fully debated and duly enacted by the Constituent Assembly of India. It took two years, eleven months and eighteen days to write and enact the Constitution.

On 26th November 1949, now celebrated as Constitution Day, the Constitution of India was adopted, making India a sovereign democratic Republic. The Constitution of India came into effect on 26th January 1950, now celebrated as Republic Day.

Dr. Rajendra Prasad became the first President of the Indian Republic, and dedicated himself to the task of nation-building. A bright set of nationalists, devoted to Gandhi's ideals of nonviolence, took up the task of nation-building and preserving our freedom. Some of these outstanding leaders deserve special mention.

DURGABAI DESHMUKH (1909-1972)

Durgabai Deshmukh was one of fifteen women elected to the Constituent Assembly for drafting the Constitution. Also India's first member of the Planning Commission, Durgabai was entirely responsible for the social welfare planning in the first Five-Year Plan of the country.

Durgabai had responded to Gandhi's call to join the freedom movement when she was in her twenties. While in jail, she took up the task of educating herself, becoming a fully qualified lawyer who began to practice along with her husband.

Uneducated and belonging to a conservative family,

Later, she played a key role in the development of the nation's Five-year Plans as part of the Central Welfare Board for Women and Children. This was Durgabai's unique contribution to the country. Alongside, she was a practicing lawyer in the Supreme Court. Durgabai was made chairperson of the Central Social Welfare Board in 1953 and was also the executive chairperson of the Population Council of India. She was also part of the United Nation's Social Defence Committee and UNESCO's International Liaison Committee for Eradication of Illiteracy (1966-1969).

"I had then decided to take up the study of law so that I could give such women free legal aid and assist them to defend themselves."

Durgabai Deshmukh, in her autobiography
Chintaman and I, 1980

LAL BAHADUR SHASTRI (1904-1966)

A devout disciple of Gandhi, Lal Bahadur Shastri became part of the Non-Cooperation Movement as a student in 1921, suffering British brutalities in prison. He joined the Uttar Pradesh government in 1947 under Govind Ballabh Pant and later headed various ministries in Nehru's cabinet.

The White Revolution, which streamlined milk production and allowed marginalized families to earn on a daily basis, was introduced during his tenure. Shastri is also credited with coining the slogan "Jai Jawan, Jai Kisan" (Hail Soldier! Hail Farmer!), which aimed at boosting the morale of the Indian Army and the farmers. He also focused on increasing production and reducing imports.

> "We would prefer to live in poverty for as long as necessary but we shall not allow our freedom to be subverted."
>
> Shastri after taking charge as the second Prime Minister of India

During his tenure, India was attacked by Pakistan in 1965. "Force will be met with force", he used these words to encourage the security forces. The Indo-Pak war ended on 23rd September 1965, after the United Nations passed a resolution demanding ceasefire. Warning against military glory and animosity between the two countries, Shastri said, "Our unique heritage, the ideals of nonviolence, truth and human brotherhood bequeathed to us by Gandhiji would be lost."

During his brief stint of two years from June 1964 to January 1966 as Prime Minister, Shastri worked on creative solutions to tackle problems like food shortage, unemployment and poverty through initiatives such as the Green Revolution, which promoted agrarian production.

In 1966, he signed the Tashkent Declaration with Pakistan President Ayub Khan in Uzbekistan, ending the 17-day Indo-Pak war. In a shocking turn of events, he died of a heart attack the same day. With him gone, India lost a promising Gandhian.

INDIRA GANDHI (1917-1984)

Being the only child of Jawaharlal Nehru who grew up in pre-independent India, Indira had developed a deep sense of patriotism for her country. She grew up witnessing the injustice that was perpetrated on Indians by the British. Swadeshi and charkha were an integral part of her growing years. As a child, she often delivered secret memos to her father's contemporaries. After marriage, she joined young socialists and even managed an underground radio station during the Quit India Movement, for which she was arrested.

After Independence, her father who was the then Prime Minister of India, groomed her in diplomacy and administration. All this made Indira qualified to manage the Congress party. In 1966, she was elected the first woman Prime Minister of India.

Indira Gandhi envisioned a modern India which could stand shoulder to shoulder with other nations but was firmly rooted in its glorious traditions and moral values of truth and peace.

Scientific progress and industrial growth figured prominently in her programmes, as she was given the mammoth task of ensuring sufficient resources for the huge population of India. She was responsible for launching various schemes to eradicate poverty, and was also credited with abolishing the unfair system of bonded labour from society.

In world affairs, she stood up for human rights issues, acquiring a prominent position among world leaders. As the Chairperson of the League of Nonaligned Nations, Indira Gandhi stood for peace and harmony in a world grappling with war and conflict.

In 1984, her phenomenal life came to a sudden end when she was assassinated by her own bodyguards.

JAYAPRAKASH NARAYAN (1902-1979)

A hero of the Quit India Movement, Jayaprakash Narayan devoted himself to rural development after Independence. Affectionately known as Loknayak or JP, he withdrew from politics and concentrated on peaceful social regeneration. JP aimed at uprooting corruption from India in tune with the principles of sarvodaya, meaning welfare of all. For this, he focused on rural reconstruction and upliftment. He stressed on people's government at the local level, focusing on democracy at the village, panchayat or block level.

JP revitalized the political landscape of the 1970s by leading a mass movement for a total revolution – social, political, economic, ideological and spiritual – with the aim of overthrowing the Congress government led by Indira Gandhi. He felt that social and political degeneration was taking root in Indian politics. He wanted to work towards a progressive India.

INTEGRATION OF PRINCELY STATES

The British left a fragmented nation. The transfer of power led to the division of two major blocks, creating space for dissonance. When India became free on 15th August 1947, it resembled an old, expensive shawl which was full of holes. In India's case, these holes were the princely states. It was necessary to integrate them with India to form one uniform nation. There were about 600 such big and small princely states that were left on their own to decide their future.

Sardar Vallabhbhai Patel, who was the Home Minister then, had to come to grips with this tremendous task. While some kings chose to join India, the people of a few other states rose against their rulers, forcing them to join India. Many of these maharajas and nawabs were convinced by Patel and his colleagues to join India. In the case of Hyderabad, violent razakars were killing and looting innocent people, and established a reign of terror with the backing of the Nizam. The Indian army was directed by the leadership to enter Hyderabad and control the razakars, ultimately forcing the Nizam to yield control and become part of India.

In the case of Kashmir, when the princely state was attacked by Pakistan, the Indian Army entered the territory to drive away the intruders. The Indian Army was called in after Maharaja Hari Singh signed the Instrument of Accession (IoA) on 26th October 1947, in which Jammu and Kashmir joined the union of India.

Thus, by the end of 1948, India was one nation with two exceptions on its map: Pondicherry, which was occupied by the French, and Goa, which was still being ruled strongly by the Portuguese.

The French left Pondicherry in 1954 after holding successful negotiations with the Government of India, bowing down to the people's wish for independence. However, the Goans had to struggle longer. The Portuguese did not believe in a peaceful settlement and continued their reign of oppression. Popular uprisings by the people of Goa and efforts of peaceful satyagrahis from other parts of India between 1954 and 1956 were ruthlessly crushed by the foreign ruler. Many of the satyagrahi women were tortured in the jails of Goa. Those considered more vocal and popular were sent by the Portuguese to jails in Lisbon, Portugal.

When all efforts to reach a peaceful settlement failed, the Indian Army entered Goa and liberated the state from the shackles of Portuguese dictatorship on 19th December 1961.

"Little pools of water tend to become stagnant and useless, but if they are joined together to form a big lake the atmosphere is cooled and there is universal benefit."

Sardar Vallabhbhai Patel, 1948

INDUSTRIAL DEVELOPMENT

Post-independence, India devoted its resources to fight poverty, develop and prosper and become self-reliant. Engineers and workers constructed huge dams and factories, which became the temples of modern India. Indian scientists made great efforts to transfer science and technology from laboratories to factories and farms.

India believed science should be used for constructive progress and not for destroying the world. Jawaharlal Nehru, along with other leaders of non-aligned nations, worked for world peace through the Non-Aligned Movement. India, with its tradition of peace and nonviolence, was holding the torch for world peace and universal brotherhood.

To involve people in the task of nation building, the country adopted a democratic system of government. The states were formed on a linguistic basis, so that people could participate in administration at the local and state level.

But in practice this was far more challenging. Instead of using language as an instrument to unite and involve people in the government, some politicians started creating divisions on the basis of linguistic preferences. Riots and violent protests erupted now and then and threatened the unity of the country.

Another major challenge was religious differences. India's democratic system ensured all religions and faiths coexist in peace and harmony. The Constitution allows us the freedom to preach and practice the religion of our choice, thus

eliminating the bias of intolerance and prejudice.

The cultural diversity, which includes differences of language, religion, cuisine and attire, make India a vibrant democracy that must be preserved at all costs. The only evils worth fighting for are poverty, backwardness and ignorance.

Right from the time of the Vedas, Indians have believed in the universality of the human spirit. Many of our great thinkers propounded the fact that the atma or soul is pure in all living beings. India's future must be guided by the philosophies of Buddha, Nanak, Vivekananda and Gandhi, who preached universal brotherhood and love and compassion for all.

Gandhi's methods of political mobilization continue to influence independence and social reform movements across the globe, giving the fight for freedom a whole new meaning.

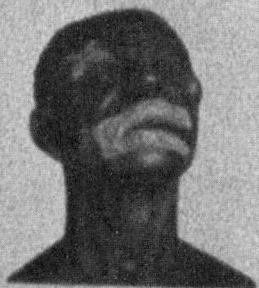

The British decision to grant freedom to India arose primarily out of necessity. But it was Gandhi's successful social movements that inspired a fundamental change in the perceptions of the colonizer, eventually leading to the collapse of the British empire. The British Raj had been the keystone of the great arc of empire from South Africa to Egypt, and Rangoon to Hong Kong. With India gaining freedom, Britain's other colonies also got liberated one after the other. The end of British rule in India, just as Winston Churchill had feared, was the beginning of the end in other colonies as well:

"And not by eastern windows only,
When the daylight comes,
comes in the light;
In front the sun climbs slow, how slowly!
But westward, look, the land is bright!"

English poet Arthur Hugh Clough,
Say Not the Struggle Naught Availeth, 1855

The same year that India gained freedom, the British announced the decision to withdraw from Palestine, followed by Burma in 1948. In 1954, Churchill declared the withdrawal of British troops from Egypt after seventy-two years of rule. Suez was next. Even though the British were adamant to keep the British garrison in the Suez canal, Egyptian President Gamal Abdel Nasser seized the vital water route in 1955, leaving the British with no option but to exit.

In 1957, the Gold Coast (now called Ghana) became independent, followed by Nigeria in 1960. African nationalist leaders such as Kwame Nkrumah in the British colony of the Gold Coast were inspired by Gandhi's success. After returning home from America, Nkrumah became the leader of the Convention Peoples' Party in 1949 and advocated the need for self-government. He began a campaign of positive action, involving nonviolent protests, strikes and non-cooperation with the British colonial authorities.

GANDHI'S GIFT TO THE WORLD

Even though the British decolonization triggered its own set of problems, particularly in Africa, it awakened a national consciousness. People who had lived under subjugation for centuries eventually overcame this oppression and emerged supreme.

King and James Bevel to adopt Gandhi's nonviolent methods in their civil rights campaigns for African-Americans. Another such example is Cesar Chavez's nonviolent campaigns for farm workers in the 1960s in California. Czechoslovakia's nonviolent defence against the Soviet occupation in

The winds of change marked the end of imperialism.
The battle Mahatma Gandhi fought all his life had finally been won.

Nonviolence aims to bring about social change, which not only rejects violence but also sees civil resistance as an alternative to passive acceptance of injustice.

The successful nonviolent struggle against British rule in India showed the light to the world. It inspired Martin Luther

1968, and the peaceful "Velvet Revolution" in 1989 saw the overthrow of the Communist government in the country. More recently, Leymah Roberta Gbowee and the women of Liberia were able to achieve peace after a 14-year-long civil war.

"If humanity is to progress, Gandhi is inescapable. He lived, thought, and acted, inspired by the vision of humanity evolving toward a world of peace and harmony. We may ignore him at our own risk."
Martin Luther King Jr. on Mahatma Gandhi

MARTIN LUTHER KING JR.

A leading light in the crusade for peace, Martin Luther King Jr. (1929 – 1968) was an eloquent Baptist in America who led the Civil Rights Movement from the mid-1950s until his death in 1968. He rose against the segregation of blacks (African-Americans) in America, especially in the South. Facing racial discrimination, blacks were not allowed to live in all parts of America. Even those who could afford better housing were kept out. Following the path of nonviolence and peaceful resistance, King Jr. became a compelling voice for their rights.

King Jr. came from a conservative Christian family. His father and maternal grandfather were both Baptist preachers. Even though he did not know poverty, King Jr. had experienced segregation and racism. He believed that the Civil Rights Movement should try to end injustice by appealing to the conscience of the nation.

King Jr. also learned about civil disobedience and resistance to slavery laws from the writings of the 19th-century American poet and philosopher Henry David Thoreau. He used Thoreau's ideas to fight racial injustice. From Gandhi, King Jr. learned how to build a movement based on such ideas.

Back in the 1950s in America, there were separate seats for whites,

blacks and people of colour in public transport services such as buses. In one instance, in the town of Montgomery, a black woman called Rosa Parks was asked to vacate a seat reserved for the whites. Her refusal to surrender her seat to a white caused a violent upsurge against the black population.

After what came to be known as the famous Montgomery Bus Boycott, King Jr. decided to wage a vigorous campaign against segregation. From 1956 to 1964, King Jr. was arrested 29 times for protesting against the unfair treatment of black people. He became more and more convinced that nonviolent resistance was the most potent weapon available to the oppressed in their struggle for freedom.

On 28th August 1963, an inter-racial assembly of more than 2,00,000 people gathered peaceably outside the Lincoln Memorial to demand equal justice for all citizens under the law. The main issues were "jobs, justice and peace". The marchers – black and white, young and old, rich and poor – held hands and sang the song "We Shall Overcome." It expressed their hope that black and white people would someday live in peace, equality and understanding. The crowds were uplifted by the emotional strength and prophetic quality of King Jr.'s famous "I have a dream" speech.

"I have a dream that one day on the red hills of Georgia
the sons of former slaves and the sons of former slave owners will
be able to sit together at the table of brotherhood...
"I have a dream that my four little children will one day live in a nation
where they will not be judged by the colour of their skin, but by
the content of their character.
I have a dream..."
Martin Luther King Jr, in his speech "I have a Dream", 1963

The march was a high point in the American civil rights movement.

King Jr. was able to turn protests into a crusade and translate local conflicts into moral issues of nationwide concern.

Successful in awakening the black masses and galvanizing them into action, Martin Luther King Jr. won his greatest victories by appealing to the conscience of white Americans, thus using political leverage to put pressure on the federal government in Washington.

The battle was only half won as the struggle continues to this day. Whether it is housing, education, or the political arena, many African-Americans still do not have equal rights as their white counterparts.

King Jr. was on a trip to Memphis, Tennessee, on 4th April 1968, in support of a strike by the city sanitation workers when he was killed by a sniper's bullet, ahead of his participation in the Poor People's March in Washington.

His books – *Stride Toward Freedom: The Montgomery Story* (1958), *Why We Can't Wait* (1964) and *Where Do We Go from Here: Chaos or Community?* (1967) reveal his inspiring activism.

"Nonviolence is a powerful and just weapon. Indeed, it is a weapon unique in history, which cuts without wounding and ennobles the man who wields it."

Martin Luther King Jr, in his Nobel lecture, The Quest for Peace, at Oslo University, 1964

NELSON MANDELA

In another part of the world, Rolihlahla Mandela (1918-2013), later given the name Nelson Mandela, championed the anti-apartheid campaign in South Africa. He educated people about nonviolent resistance and made it the primary tool to attain freedom and equality.

Mandela came from a proud African background. The belligerent foreign occupants had destroyed the ancient peace and harmony of Xhosa tribes in South Africa. He grew up hearing stories of valour of his ancestors during the war of resistance and dreamt of one day making his own contribution to his people's freedom.

Mandela's struggle began with his imprisonment on Robben Island, where all political prisoners were kept. The inmates had to work outdoors in an isolated lime quarry. When left to themselves in mine shafts, the prisoners discussed their views on the injustice prevailing in society and exchanged whatever knowledge they had on these issues.

Mandela held regular lectures in secret, lending the prison a spirit akin to the creative exchanges of a university. Later, the prison would be called The Robben Island University or Nelson Mandela University.

> "Fault, dear Brutus, is not in
> our stars, but in ourselves,
> that we are underlings…"
> Mandela, quoting from Shakespeare's
> Julius Caesar

Addressing the prisoners, many of whom awaited a death sentence, Mandela repeated his favourite passage:

> "Cowards die many times before
> their deaths; the valiant never
> taste of death but once."

The ideals of Gandhi were kept alive in South Africa by Mandela. Gandhi's early association with South Africa had a great impact on the sensibilities of its people. Mandela's early encounters with peace-loving Hindus and Muslims had also built a strong bond between the African National Congress (ANC) and South Africa's Indian population. The ANC turned multicultural and multi-religious, bound by a common goal. Gandhi's granddaughter Ela Gandhi, an activist and politician aligned with the ANC, described Mandela as the living legacy of Mahatma Gandhi; the Gandhi of South Africa.

After 27 years in prison, Mandela was successful in negotiating the dismantling of the apartheid regime in South Africa, leading to democratic elections. He became the first black president of the country in 1994. Reflecting on this achievement, he once stated that "the common ground is greater and more enduring than the differences that divide."

He reasoned that the democratic process must rest upon equality, pluralism and multi-ethnicity. Mandela transcended the idea of national liberty by saying no to exclusively black or tribal liberation movements, thus making space for the cause of multi-ethnicities. He was behind the most multi-ethnic government ever formed, know as the Rainbow Government, which included Africans, Europeans and Asians. In achieving this, Mandela had to agitate against black domination. He did not argue for a black-dominated glorious African society of bygone times but called for a completely new kind of state, a multi-ethnic democracy constituted by diverse cultures having equal rights.

A broad cultural and political basis marked the government of 1994. Ministers of state included blacks, whites and coloureds, and among whom were Indians, Muslims, Christians, communists, liberals and conservatives. Never had such a cabinet existed in Africa or elsewhere. Many prominent posts were occupied by either Africans or Afrikaners, all widening the arch of a rainbow nation. The Constitution of the Republic of South Africa, 1996, is one of the most modern and radical documents in the world, having human rights at its core.

Inspired by his native heritage, other freedom movements, and by drawing lessons from the history and literature of his oppressors, Mandela forged a vision of humanity that encompassed all peoples and set a fine example for the rest of the world.

In his Nobel lecture, Mandela called himself a mere representative of the millions of people across the globe who "recognized that an injury to one is an injury to all", which is the essence of ubuntu philosophy.

On 16th March 2001, India conferred the International Gandhi Peace Prize on Nelson Mandela. It was a tribute to an unusual Gandhian hero who personified the triumph of the human spirit over the forces of oppression.

"Umuntu ngumuntu ngabantu." (A person is a person through other people.)
Zulu phrase often quoted by Mandela

AUNG SAN SUU KYI

In the troubled waters of authoritarian Independent Myanmar, Aung San Suu Kyi (1945-), the youngest daughter of the martyred hero Aung San, returned to Yangon from the University of Oxford, England, in 1988, to nurse her dying mother, Khin Kyi, who was a former diplomat. In no time, she plunged into the country's nationwide pro-democracy uprising against the military regime. Joining the newly-formed National League for Democracy (NLD), Suu Kyi called for freedom and democracy. She entered politics for the democratization of her nation and assumed the leadership of her party.

> "It is not power that corrupts but fear. Fear of losing power corrupts those who wield it and fear of the scourge of power corrupts those who are subject to it."
>
> Aung San Suu Kyi, in her Nobel Prize acceptance speech, 1991

The Myanmar military responded to the uprising with brute force, killing nearly 5,000 demonstrators. Unable to maintain its grip on power, the regime was forced to call a general election in 1990.

A believer of Gandhi's nonviolence principle, Aung San Suu Kyi began to campaign for the NLD when she was detained by the regime. Despite Suu Kyi being under house arrest, the NLD went on to win a staggering 82% majority. However, the regime refused to recognize the election results.

Suu Kyi has been in and out of prison ever since. She was under house arrest from 1989-1995 and again from 2000-2002. In 2003, she was arrested after the Depayin massacre, where nearly 100 of her supporters were beaten to death by the militia. During her house arrest in 2004, her phone lines were cut and the security deployed by her party at her residence was also removed. For her courage and peaceful ways of resistance, she was awarded the Nobel Peace Prize in 1991.

However, in recent years, Suu Kyi had a fall from grace when The Gambia, backed by the Organisation of Islamic Cooperation

(OIC), filed a case at the International Court of Justice (ICJ), accusing Myanmar of committing genocide against the Rohingya minority. Interestingly, the case was filed by The Gambia, a country which had no direct connection to the alleged crimes but which used its membership to highlight human rights violations. In response, personally appearing before the ICJ, Suu Kyi asked the international court to drop the genocide case against Myanmar.

The developments have raised serious questions over the nonviolent nature of her politics and have also raised doubts over her regime.

NON-ALIGNED MOVEMENT

Across the globe, political stalwarts subscribed to the efficacy of nonviolence for settling internal social discords and also for enhancing international relations. In sharp contrast to armed defence forces such as NATO (North Atlantic Treaty Organization, 1949), SEATO (South East Asia Treaty Organization, 1954) and the Warsaw Pact (1955), the Non-Aligned Movement founded in 1961 at the Belgrade Conference became a forum of 120 developing world countries, which were not formally aligned or against any power-blocs in the Cold War. After the United Nations, NAM is the largest group of states in the world.

Under the leadership of Josip Broz Tito of Yugoslavia, Gamal Abdel Nasser of Egypt, Prime Minister Jawaharlal Nehru, Kwame Nkrumah of Ghana and Sukarno of Indonesia, NAM stood against colonialism and imperialism. Josip Broz Tito, notable for his policy of neutrality, led the communist Council of National Liberation to establish a democratic regime after deposing the royalty in Yugoslavia. Nasser, who became the first President of Egypt was a patron of socialist independence in the region. Nasser's policies emphasized on territorial integrity, non-aggression and peaceful existence. Together, Nehru, Tito and Nasser became the voice of developing countries and encouraged their concerted actions in world affairs.

RECENT MOVEMENTS

The world had found an effective system of resistance in nonviolent protests to fight evils such as racial inequality and other forms of injustice. But peaceful ways of resistance were also being used to address environmental concerns such as the risk posed by extensive mining or construction of dams. These movements also used nonviolent ways to draw the attention of governments or corporates.

The most outstanding of these was the idea of hugging trees. The Chipko Movement, under the leadership of Sunderlal Bahuguna, sought a legal ban on indiscriminate felling of trees, which often led to landslides and subsidence in the Himalayan ranges. Thanks to the efforts of the Chipko activists, the peaceful method of tree-hugging to stop the felling of trees became a symbol of environmental conservation.

This method has been used by Greenpeace activists, who in one instance lived under trees and faced severe weather conditions to save a park in Southampton, England. The activists have also been peacefully campaigning on issues of air pollution, prevention of forest fires and plastic disasters.

In America, another campaign called Saving the Bees worked for the preservation of wild habitats, warned against soil and water erosion and urged that the use of chemical fertilizers and pesticides be minimized. Acting on a cause long advocated by Greenpeace, Mexico, Bhutan and eight European countries imposed a ban on genetically modified (GM) crops. From Sweden, a young environmental activist called Greta Thunberg criticised world leaders for their failure to act in the face of the climate change crisis.

"So everyone out there, it is now time for civil disobedience, it is time to rebel."
Greta Thunberg on the climate change crisis, at the Declaration of Rebellion, Parliament Square, London, 2018

Greta Thunberg

Meanwhile, two Nobel Peace Prize sensations Kailash Satyarthi and Malala Yousafzai also made a difference through their peaceful ways of resistance. Satyarthi instituted the Kailash Satyarthi Children's Foundation in India to fight for child rights in India. He found peaceful ways of fighting child labour, slavery and trafficking. Satyarthi is responsible for liberating thousands of children from child labour and providing education to many more.

The young Malala Yousafzai, in Pakistan, also championed the cause of every child's right to education. Both Satyarthi and Malala envisioned a world where children are free, safe and have equal opportunity to realise their potential.

Malala Yousafzai

In recent times, amidst the raging pandemic, an African-American called George Floyd was arrested by Minneapolis police on account of an alleged "forgery in process", and was brutally suffocated to death under the pressure of a white policeman's knee. Floyd's last words were, "I can't breath". Floyd's death triggered an upsurge of antipathy towards cops throughout America and the rest of the world, underlining the fact that black lives matter. The unfortunate incident led to better awareness about racial inequality, safety, right to education and medical care. Silent nonviolent marches in various parts of America paid tribute to Floyd, and came to be known as the "I Can't Breathe" Movement.

The spirit of man, from the beginning of time, has striven for freedom and equality. Freedom is being accepted for one's way of thinking, and the understanding and acceptance of an individual's beliefs by others. It can be expressed in the simplest of things. Expressions such as tattoos, piercing, or any other fashion statement are ways to exercise one's personal freedom, without limiting the actions and thoughts of others or violating their rights. Both freedom and equality are mutually dependent. Without freedom, equality is meaningless; and without equality, there will be no real freedom.

> "Without freedom of thought, there can be no such thing as wisdom – and no such thing as public liberty without freedom of speech..."
>
> Benjamin Franklin, 1722

In recent times, the legal rights of lesbian, gay, bi-sexual and transgender (LGBT) people the world over have gained social acceptance. In a historic judgement, Menaka Guruswamy and Arundhati Katju battled on social and legal fronts for their fundamental right to privacy, dignity and love in a same sex marriage, overturning the 157-year-old law Section 377 IPC. The landmark judgement by the Supreme Court in 2018 ruled in favour of humanity by unanimously decriminalizing homosexuality. The LGBTQ community across the world has battled on both legal and social fronts for decades – for their fundamental rights to privacy, dignity, safety and love.

A world icon for music and style, Lady Gaga is openly bi-sexual and the driving force behind the Born This Way Foundation, which is striving to build a kinder and braver world. Among some noted campaigners of LGBTQ rights is transgender icon Marsha P. Johnson who fought for the dignity of their creed and co-founded the

Lady Gaga

Street Transvestite Action Revolutionaries (STAR) to provide housing for queer youth and sex workers in Lower Manhattan. Edith Windsor, a technology manager with IBM, became the lead plaintiff in 2013 to overturn the US laws for the same sex marriage movement, extending rights, privileges and benefits to same-sex couples. Another activist for the LGBTQ movement, is Peter Gray Tatchell, contested British elections for the Labour Party, and stressed on the need for freedom to make personal choices in a free world.

People across the world demand the realization of diverse rights to ensure their individual and collective well-being. These human rights ensure freedom, dignity and justice for the people, regardless of their colour, place of birth, ethnicity, race, religion or sex. People seek guarantee and protection by the State without distinction.

when two Portuguese students were jailed just for raising a toast to freedom. He wrote an article in *The Observer* newspaper and launched a campaign that provoked an incredible response. Reprinted in newspapers across the world, his call to action sparked the idea that people everywhere can unite in solidarity for justice and freedom. Through the years,

"We the peoples of United Nations determined to save succeeding generations from the scourge of war, which twice in our lifetime has brought untold sorrow to mankind, and to reaffirm faith in fundamental human rights, in the dignity and worth of the human person, in the equal rights of men and women and of nations large and small, and to establish conditions under which justice and respect for the obligations arising from treaties and other sources of international law can be maintained, and to promote social progress and better standards of life in larger freedom..."

Preamble of the United Nations Charter

In July 1961, Amnesty International was formed in London by British lawyer Peter Benenson to bring human rights abuses to people's attention. He was outraged

the organization has attracted membership from nations across the globe, emphasizing their role in restoring harmony, justice and peace.

NONVIOLENCE TODAY

One of the challenges that the world faces today is the pervasiveness of violence. The quest for peace that goes beyond the mere absence of war, must include justice and compassion, human rights and responsibilities, and celebration of diversity.

More than ever, the ideals of freedom and nonviolence are needed as the guiding light for a better world. For those striving for justice, the principle of satyagraha can provide the strength to practice non-cooperation without ill will towards their oppressor. The virtues of nonviolence and satyagraha imbue in the practitioner a readiness to understand even the most unpleasant stand of an opponent.

Even though nonviolent satyagraha takes longer to bear fruit, it causes less damage to people and property and does not perpetuate the cycle of hatred and revenge. In any action led by ahimsa, truth is the ultimate goal. And truth always shows the light to victory.

उद्वयं तमसस्परि ज्योतिस् पश्चन्तोउत्तरम्

देवान देवत्र सुर्यमगमन ज्योतिर्

ऋग्वेद

Gazing beyond the dark we reach the Supreme light and
Attain the Sun, the God of Gods, the Light.
Rig Veda

◆ ◆ ◆

GLOSSARY

Charkha	Mahatma Gandhi chose the charkha or spinning wheel as an important tool for political emancipation, and as a symbol of economic and social reaction to British Rule.
Mahatma	Mahatma was a title Gandhi's followers bestowed on him, that meant a higher soul, or "Great Soul".
Partition	The Partition of India took place in August 1947 when the country was granted independence from the rule of the British empire and was divided into two: India and Pakistan.
Satyagraha	Meaning holding firmly to the truth, Satyagraha was Gandhi's idea of nonviolent protest – a form of passive resistance. The person who practices Satyagraha is a satyagrahi.
Swaraj	Swaraj was Gandhi's idea of self-rule, or home rule, for India, in which Indians ruled themselves.
Purna Swaraj	Purna Swaraj or 'total independence' was a historic resolution that was passed by the Indian National Congress on 19th December 1929 at its Lahore session. A public declaration was made on 26th January 1930.
Swadeshi Movement	During the freedom struggle, the Swadeshi movement was a people's movement that sought to encourage the use of Indian-made items, particularly cottage-industry products, such as hand-loomed cloth, and to oppose British-made goods.

YOUR IDEA OF FREEDOM

List down the freedoms you are thankful for in your life.

_____

_____

_____

_____

_____

At the national / global level, which freedoms are we yet to achieve?

_____

_____

_____

_____

_____

Is there such a thing as too much freedom?

_____

_____

_____

_____

_____

PICTURE CREDITS

The Man Who Changed it All: Wikimedia Commons. Author Unknown; Source: www. gandhiserve.org

The Non-Cooperation Movement: Wikimedia Commons, Author Unknown; Source: https:// www.architecturaldigest.in/content/gandhi-jayanti-iconic-photos-mahatma/

The Dandi March: Wikimedia Commons, Author: Yann

The Torchbearer: Wikimedia Commons, Author Unknown; Source: http://www.columbia.edu/ itc/mealac/pritchett/00routesdata/1900_1999/partition/sardarpatel/sardarpatel.html

Second World War: Wikimedia Commons, Author: Captain Richard Birdwood; Source: United Kingdom Government; Source: https://collection.nam.ac.uk/detail.php?acc=1951-12-25-136

Quit India: Wikimedia Commons, Author Unknown; Source: http://www.columbia.edu/itc/ mealac/pritchett/00routesdata/1800_1899/congress/nehru/withgandhi1942.jpg

Freedom at Last! Wikimedia Commons, Author Unknown; Source: http://www.columbia.edu/ itc/mealac/pritchett/00routesdata/1900_1999/partition/trains/trains.html

The Constitution of India: Wikimedia Commons, Author Unknown; Source: http://www. outlookindia.com/printarticle.aspx?290562

Other Freedoms: Wikimedia Commons, Author: Rob Bogaerts / Anefo; Source: http://proxy. handle.net/10648/ad6b1b46-d0b4-102d-bcf8-003048976d84

The authors would like to acknowledge the following for enriching their perspective during the making of this book.

1. Chandra B, Tripathi A, and De B, *Freedom Struggle*, NBT, New Delhi.

2. Bolitho H, *Jinnah: The Creator of Pakistan*, John Murray Publishers Ltd, 1954

3. Louis F, *The Life of Mahatma Gandhi*, Granada Publishers, 1982

4. Majumdar RC, *History of Freedom Movement in India*, South Asia Books, 1988

5. Gandhi MK, *My Experiments with Truth*, Navajivan Trust, 1927

6. Majumdar RC, *Struggle for Freedom*, Bharatiya Vidya Bhavan, 1969

7. Majumdar RC, *British Paramountcy & Indian Resistance*, Bharatiya Vidya Bhavan, 2011

8. Majumdar RC, *The Sepoy Mutiny and the Revolt of 1857*, Calcutta, Firma KL Mukhopadhyay, 1963

9. Nehru J, *The Discovery of India*, Signet Press, 1946

10. Nehru J, *Glimpses of World History*, Oxford University Press, 1989

11. Sharma SR, *India in History (III)*, Orient Longman

12. Gandhi MK, *The Law of Love*, Bharatiya Vidya Bhawan, 1970

13. Chand T, *History of Freedom Movement in India*, Publications Division, 1961

14. Sharma SL, *India Freedom Struggle Centenary (1857-1957): Souvenir*, 1957

15. Collins L, Lapierre D, *Freedom at Midnight*, Vikas Publishing, 2011

16. Herman A, *Gandhi and Churchill: The Rivalry That Destroyed An Empire and Forged Our Age*, 2009.

17. Anon, *One Hundred Great Lives*, Odhams Press, London, 1948

18. Tendulkar D.G, *Mahatma: Life of Mohandas Karamchand Gandhi*, volumes 1-8, Vithalbhai K. Jhaveri & D.G. Tendulkar; 1951

19. 54th Adhiveshan Rashtriya Mahasabha, Meerut, 1946.

ACKNOWLEDGEMENTS

From the bottom of our hearts, we express our grateful and respectful thanks to:

- All those freedom fighters we approached to gain first-hand insights into their aspirations for freedom, and their role in using nonviolence as a moral force against the brute force of the British rule.

- Our dear colleague Late Surekha Panandiker, who worked with us in researching and creating the book, *Triumph of Nonviolence*. Her deep understanding of the subject helped us in describing many historical events in the book in a concise and vivid manner. While working on the manuscript, Surekha kept our spirits high with her rich ideas and interesting anecdotes.

- Tina Narang, Publisher – Children's, HarperCollins India, for seeing potential in this book and accepting it for publication. We are fortunate to have worked with a thorough professional, and in the process have gained a charming and enthusiastic friend. We shall be forever indebted to her for her keen insight.

- A very friendly and thorough Medha Gupta, Associate Editor, HarperCollins India, who has painstakingly helped in sharpening the facts and the text. Her deep understanding of the subject and way of presentation added to the book's charm.

- The talented Arun Pottirayil, whose imaginative compositions and bold line drawings enliven the text, and the immensely creative designer Sukriti Sobti whose layout and design uplifted the pages.

- The eminent authors, journalists, politicians and proficient literati for their thoughts and kind words of encouragement.

ABOUT THE AUTHORS

A child psychologist, writer and critic of children's books, **Ira Saxena** has written fiction and non-fiction in Hindi and English for children of all ages and adults. Her writings are mostly based on themes such as computer crime, science fiction and Gandhism.

She received the Shankar's Silver Medal for Writing in 1996 for *Gajmukta ki Talaash (Quest for the Jumbo Pearl)* – an adventure set in India's freedom struggle, and also won the White Raven's selection at the International Youth Library in 2000 for her computer crime novel *The Virus Trap*. Many of her short stories have been awarded by publications such as *Amar Chitra Katha* and *Saptahik Hindustan*. Her books have found a place in schools as supplementary readers. Her recent novels include *Curse of Grass*, *The Web Trail*, *Chand Katori* and *Paraa*.

Saxena is the founding member and Secretary of the Association of Writers and Illustrators for Children (AWIC). She has also been a member of the International Board on Books for Young People (IBBY). A firm believer in the healing touch of literature, Saxena is spearheading a book therapy project among teachers and authors. She can be reached at saxena.ira@gmail.com

◆ ◆ ◆

Nilima Sinha is a well-known author for children, who has written several award-winning books, such as *The Chandipur Jewels* which won a Best Fiction award and *The Yellow Butterfly* which received a Best Picture book award. Her books have been included in the International White Ravens catalogue by the International Youth Library. She writes in both English and Hindi.

Sinha has worked on the Marigold series produced by NCERT as English textbooks for schools in India. Her book, *Hamirpur ke Khandahar* was prescribed as a Supplementary Reader in Hindi for all government schools in the Delhi region. Her schooling at the Convent of Jesus and Mary, New Delhi, inspired her interest in literary writing.

She is the President of the Association of Writers and Illustrators for Children (AWIC), the Indian branch of the International Board on Books for Young People (IBBY). In the past, she has also held the post of Vice-President of IBBY. She can be reached at sinhan2008@gmail.com

ABOUT THE ILLUSTRATOR

Arun Pottirayil is an illustrator with more than twenty years of experience in digital and hand-drawn illustrations. A self-taught artist with a passion for illustrating, Pottirayil previously worked with Dorling Kindersley, mostly illustrating for DK Eyewitness Travel guides. He is a post graduate in English Literature from Government Victoria College, Kerala.

ABOUT THE DESIGNER

Sukriti Sobti is a graphic designer with several years of experience in the book publishing industry. Currently based in Vancouver, Canada, Sobti has previously worked with publishing houses such as Dorling Kindersley and has been creating and designing content for children. She has a Master's Degree in English Literature from Jamia Milia Islamia and a Post-graduate Diploma in Graphics and Animation from the same university.